THE PALESTINIANS: CURRENT ISSUES AND HISTORICAL BACKGROUND

The Palestinians: Current Issues and Historical Background

Clyde Mark, Kenneth Katzman,
Carol Migdalovitz, Alfred Prados
and Joshua Ruebner

Nova Science Publishers, Inc.
New York

Senior Editors: Susan Boriotti and Donna Dennis
Coordinating Editor: Tatiana Shohov
Office Manager: Annette Hellinger
Graphics: Wanda Serrano
Editorial Production: Marius Andronie, Vladimir Klestov, Matthew Kozlowski,
Tom Moceri, Anthony T. Sovak and Maya Columbus
Circulation: Ave Maria Gonzalez, Vera Popovich, Luis Aviles, Melissa Diaz,
Magdalene Nunez, Marlene Nunez and Jeannie Pappas
Communications and Acquisitions: Serge P. Shohov
Marketing: Cathy DeGregory

Library of Congress Cataloging-in-Publication Data
Available Upon Request

ISBN: 1-59033-609-7.

400 Oser Ave, Suite 1600
Hauppauge, New York 11788-3619
Tele. 631-231-7269 Fax 631-231-8175
e-mail: Novascience@earthlink.net
Web Site: http://www.novapublishers.com

Printed in the United States of America

CONTENTS

PREFACE

Between World War II and the collapse of the Soviet union, U.S. policy toward the Middle East was based on several broad goals, the most noteworthy of which were (1) stop Soviet expansion into the region; (2) keep open the Middle Eastern lines of communication and trade; (3) maintain Western access to Middle Eastern oil; (4) foster democracy and free trade market economies; and (5) protect Israel's security. This book presents current issues concerning the Palestinians as well as a historical background.

Chapter 1

PALESTINIANS AND MIDDLE EAST PEACE: ISSUES FOR THE UNITED STATES

Clyde Mark

INTRODUCTION

The United States began contacts with the Palestine Liberation Organization (PLO) in December 1988, after the PLO accepted Israel's right to exist, accepted U.N. Resolutions 242 and 338 that call for an exchange of land for peace, and renounced terrorism. The United States continues its contacts with the PLO and the Palestinian Authority elected in January 1996, and is an active broker in the continuing Middle East peace process.

Congress gave the President the authority to waive previously passed legislation prohibiting U.S. contributions to the United Nations from funding any PLO activities, threatening to withdraw U.S. membership from international organizations that recognize the PLO, prohibiting U.S. government employees from negotiating with the PLO, and labeling the PLO a terrorist organization. The waiver authority was extended in P.L. 104-107 (February 12, 1996), but expired August 12, 1997. Congress also ordered closed PLO offices in Washington and New York, although the New York office serving the U.N. remains open under a U.S. court decision.

In opening remarks to the Madrid conference on October 30, 1991, the Palestinian delegation accepted transitional phases for the peace process and accepted confederation of a Palestinian state with Jordan. Despite accepting confederation, most Palestinians want an independent Palestinian state.

The Israeli and Palestinian delegations did not appear to be making any progress in resolving any of the issues: elections for an interim Palestinian administration, the future national status of the West Bank and Gaza Strip, borders, peacekeeping forces, demilitarized zones, water and natural resource sharing, population exchanges, economic cooperation, diplomatic relations, and the status of Jerusalem. Then on August 19, 1993, Israeli and PLO representatives initialed a secretly arranged Declaration of Principles to guide future negotiations. On September 10, the PLO and Israel exchanged letters of mutual recognition, and on September 13, the two signed the Declaration of Principles, that called for Israeli withdrawal from Gaza and Jericho, the election of a Palestinian Council, and negotiations for future withdrawals and a permanent settlement in 5 years.

On May 4, 1994, Israel and the PLO signed an agreement providing for the Israeli withdrawal from Gaza and Jericho (withdrawal completed May 11, 1994). The Interim Agreement signed on September 28, 1995 (also called Oslo II or the Taba Agreement), provided for elections for the 88-seat Palestinian Assembly, the release of Israeli-held prisoners, Israeli withdrawal from six West Bank cities, and other issues. The Israelis withdrew from the West Bank cities by the end of 1995, and the Palestinian Assembly was elected on January 20, 1996, and sworn in on March 7, 1996.

Israel and the Palestinians agreed to an Israeli withdrawal from Hebron in January 1997, and on October 23, 1998 signed the Wye agreement to meet previous commitments. The peace talks stalled at Camp David in July 2000, and remain suspended since the Palestinian uprising began in September. Some 1,493 Palestinians and 585 Israelis have died in the continuing confrontation.

Most Recent Developments

On April 8, 2003, President Arafat extended by two weeks the time for Prime Minister-designate Mahmud Abbas to form a cabinet. According to press reports, Arafat and Abbas disagree over who should be Interior Minister, Arafat appointee Hani al-Hassan or Abbas choice Muhammad Dahlan. Arafat appointed Abbas (aka Abu Mazen) to be Prime Minister on March 6, 2003. Creating a prime minister to share power with Arafat or to replace him was one of several reforms advocated by the United States, Israel, and others.

In President Bush's March 25, 2003 supplemental appropriations request, the West Bank and Gaza are slated to receive $50 million in Economic Support Funds for civil reform, humanitarian relief, water resource development, and other programs.

As of April 9, 2003, 1,982 Palestinians and 727 Israelis have died in the fighting since September 2000.

BACKGROUND AND ANALYSIS

The United States and the Palestinians

U.S. Policy toward the Palestinians

Between World War II and the 1991 collapse of the Soviet Union, U.S. policy toward the Middle East was based on several broad goals, the most noteworthy of which were (1) stop Soviet expansion into the region; (2) keep open the Middle Eastern lines of communication and trade; (3) maintain Western access to Middle Eastern oil; (4) foster democracy and free market economies; and (5) protect Israel's security.

There appear to be many reasons why U.S. citizens have favored Israel: Israel and the United States espouse shared Judeo-Christian principles; both countries were "pioneering" in their early years; both countries are democracies; the United States has empathy for Israel's position as an embattled "underdog"; Israel and the United States opposed Soviet expansion during the cold war years; the United States has sympathy for the experience of European Jews in World War II; Jewish-Americans have a very effective pro-Israel political support organization; and the United States is more aware of Israel's point of view. In short, Israelis "are like us." Conversely, there is less empathy among Americans for Arab viewpoints because Arabs are "not like us." Eastern Arab culture (dress, food, music, art, written and spoken language, religion) appears to have little in common with Western American culture, and Arab-Americans in the past have tended to assimilate more than some other ethnic groups and to avoid the public stage of advocacy for Arab causes.

Refugees and Terrorists

The United States, until recently, treated the Palestinians as one of the problems to be solved in ending the Arab-Israeli dispute rather than as participants in the peace process. From 1948 until the 1967 war, the United States, like many other countries, considered the Palestinian people in the context of the refugee problem and not as an independent national movement. Beginning with a series of terrorist incidents starting in 1968, most added "terrorist" to the "refugee" image of Palestinians. President Carter shifted the terrorist-refugee perception on March 16, 1977, when he said the Palestinians deserved a homeland, and on January 4, 1978, when he said that the Palestinians had legitimate rights and should participate in any deliberations about their future. The Camp David agreements of September 1978 mentioned "the legitimate rights of the Palestinian people." Early in the Reagan Administration, officials returned to referring to Palestinians as "refugees" and "terrorists" and did not mention Palestinian rights or self-determination. But in his September 1, 1982, Middle East address, President Reagan said that the Palestinian problem was more than refugees.

Recognition

The United States changed its policy toward the PLO in 1988. In 1975, one year after the Arab League stated that the Palestine Liberation Organization (PLO) was the sole representative of the Palestinian people, Secretary of State Henry Kissinger informed Israel that the United States would not recognize or negotiate with the PLO unless and until the PLO recognized Israel and accepted U.N. Resolutions 242 and 338. Congress codified the pledge into law (Section 535, P.L. 98-473, October 12, 1984), and added that the PLO also must renounce terrorism. PLO chairman Yasir Arafat told the U.N. General Assembly meeting in Geneva (because the United States would not grant Arafat a visa to attend the U.N. session in New York) that the PLO recognized Israel, accepted U.N. Resolutions 242 and 338, and renounced terrorism. Secretary of State George Shultz stated on December 14, 1988, that the PLO had met the conditions stipulated by the United States, and that the United States would open a dialogue with the PLO in Tunis, Tunisia, on December 16, 1988. It was not made public why the Reagan Administration, considered by most to be pro-Israeli, chose to open the dialogue with the PLO at that time. Some speculate that President-elect George Bush asked President Reagan for the gesture as part of a Bush plan to address the Arab-Israeli issue.

The United States maintained the dialogue with the PLO in Tunis until June 20, 1990, when President Bush ended the talks because the PLO did not denounce an attempted terrorist attack near Tel Aviv on May 30, 1990. President Bush announced on March 6, 1991 (in the wake of the Gulf war), that he would pursue Arab-Israeli peace negotiations; he dispatched Secretary of State Baker to the Middle East where he met with Palestinian leaders from the occupied territories. Baker's 8 trips to the region and his contacts with the Palestinians, Jordanians, Israelis, Syrians, Egyptians, and others led to peace talks in Madrid on October 30, 1991. But at Madrid and the subsequent meetings, the United States (and

Israel) treated the Palestinians as part of the Jordanian delegation, not as a separate entity.

On September 10, 1993, following the Israeli-PLO mutual recognition, President Clinton announced that the United States would resume the dialogue with the PLO. PLO leader Arafat, representing the national aspirations of the Palestinian people, shared the spotlight with Israeli Prime Minister Rabin and President Clinton at the signing of the Declaration of Principles on the White House lawn on September 13, 1993. U.S. official attitudes toward the Palestinians had evolved from seeing them only as refugees to according them a form of recognition that approached, but did not reach, nationhood. Following a pledge made at the Wye River conference, President Clinton visited Gaza to attend the December 14, 1998 meeting of the PLO National Council, at which the Council voted by show of hands to reaffirm that the PLO Covenant had been amended to remove anti-Israeli references.

Current Relations

The White House refuses to meet with Palestinian President Yasir Arafat because, in the Administration's view, Arafat is not doing enough to stop terrorism.

U.S. Aid for the Palestinians

(See Table 4, U.S. Assistance to the West Bank and Gaza, at the end of this report)

At an October 1, 1993, Washington meeting, 46 donor nations pledged $2.4 billion for the Palestinian entity. The U.S. Administration offered $500 million ($125 million in loans or loan guarantees and $375 million in grants) over 5 years for economic development of the Palestinian entity. Of the $125 million available in loan guarantees, only $3 million had been drawn through April 2001. The United States provided only $36 million funding for the Palestinian Authority through the Holst Fund of the World Bank. The remaining $339 million was delivered through private voluntary organizations (PVOs), and through USAID contracts. No U.S. aid went directly to the PLO.

Wye Agreement Funding

On November 30, 1998, President Clinton told the donors conference in Washington that the United States would provide $400 million in grants for the Palestinians, $200 million of which would be provided in FY1999, $100 million in FY2000, and $100 million in FY2001. (The President also requested $1.2 billion for Israel and $300 million for Jordan to implement the Wye Agreement.)

Congress did not include funding for the Wye Agreement in the Foreign Operations Appropriations bills for FY2000 (H.R. 2606, S. 1234). The President vetoed H.R. 2606 in part because it did not contain funding for the Wye Agreement. After negotiations with the White House, the House of Representatives passed H.R. 3196 on November 5, 1999, that included the Wye Agreement funding; $1.2 billion for Israel, $200 million for Jordan, $25 million for Egypt, and $400 million for the Palestinians. H.R. 3196 was set aside and replaced with H.R. 3422, which was included by reference in H.R. 3194, the consolidated appropriations bill passed by the House on November 18, by the Senate on November 19, and presented to the President on November 22, 1999. The $400 million Wye supplemental was in addition to annual aid levels of about $75 million.

According to a State Department report presented to Congress in late October 1999, the Wye funding for the Palestinians would be spent as follows:

Palestinians: $400 million

$100 million — Community Development (health, education, water, infrastructure, services)

$30 million — Rule of Law (law enforcement, human rights, train judges, prosecutors, lawyers, etc.)

$10 million — Industrial Estate - West Bank

$100 million — Gaza Port, Gaza-West Bank passageway

$30 million — Scholarship Fund

$100 million — Janin-Nablus Road

$30 million — Contingency Fund

As of December 2002, $158 million of the $400 million was yet to be obligated, according to the Department of State. It is assumed that the $158 million will be spent in FY2003.

Other Assistance

On November 14, 2000, President Clinton requested an emergency appropriation that included an unspecified amount for FY2002 for the Palestinians to be drawn from $150 million to be shared among Egypt, Jordan, and the Palestinians. The request submitted to Congress also included $450 million for Israel, $225 million for Egypt, and $75 million for Jordan for FY2001, and an additional $350 million for Israel for FY2002. The 106th Congress adjourned without acting on the request.

The supplemental appropriation for FY2002 (H.R. 4775, P.L. 107-206, signed on August 2, 2002) includes $50 million in disaster relief assistance for the Palestinians, primarily in response to damages inflicted during the April-May 2002 Israeli military operations in Palestinian areas, particularly the city of Jenin. The section specifically allocates the funds for the West Bank and Gaza and prohibits funding for the Palestinian Authority.

Congress and the PLO

Congress stated its opposition to the U.N. special committee on Palestinian rights (Section 614, P.L. 95-426, October 7, 1978), opposed U.S. participation in the International Monetary Fund if the IMF granted membership to the PLO (Section 7, P.L. 96-389, October 7, 1980), and stated that U.S. funds contributed to the U.N. could not be used to support the PLO (Section 154, P.L. 97-377, December 21, 1982). In 1984, Congress prohibited U.S. government employees from negotiating with or recognizing the PLO unless and until the PLO recognized Israel's right to exist, accepted U.N. Resolutions 242 and 338, and renounced terrorism (Section 535, P.L. 98- 473, October 12, 1984).

In 1987, Congress declared the PLO to be a terrorist organization and a threat to U.S. interests, and ordered the PLO information office in Washington and the office of the PLO U.N. mission in New York to be closed (Title X of P.L. 100-204, December 22, 1987). The Department of State closed the Washington office, but the New York office remained open after a judge ruled that the office was legal under the U.N. treaty signed by the United States. The Washington office reopened in September 1993, after the PLO and Israel signed the Declaration of Principles under waiver provisions in the Middle East Peace Facilitation Act. The PLO office closed on August 12, 1997, when the Middle East Peace Facilitation Act expired because the presidential waiver expired with the act. The PLO office reopened on December 6, 1997, when the President exercised the waiver in Section 539(d) of P.L. 105-118, the foreign operations appropriations law. The office remained open under subsequent presidential waivers provided in the foreign operations appropriations bills. The Foreign Operations Appropriations bill (H.R. 5410/S. 2779) currently in conference provides for a 6-month waiver in Section 534(d). According to April 2002 press reports, the PLO was evicted from its Washington office because it could not pay the rent.

In 1989, Congress added Title VIII, the PLO**Error! Bookmark not defined.** Commitments Compliance Act (PLOCCA), to P.L. 101-246, signed into law on February 16, 1990, which repeated the prohibition against negotiating with the PLO, stated the sense of Congress that the United States should seek to prevent PLO involvement in terrorism, said the United States should obtain an accounting from the PLO of several listed incursions into Israel, required the Secretary of State to report to the Congress on the PLO explanation of the incursions, and required the President to file quarterly reports on several listed PLO activities and positions. The Secretary of State sent the first PLO Compliance Act report to Congress on January 11, 1994, stating that the PLO remained opposed to terrorism and that the United States would continue the dialogue resumed on September 10, 1993.

Following the signing of the Declaration of Principles on September 13, 1993, Congress passed the Middle East Peace Facilitation Act (MEPFA) granting the President the authority to waive sections of existing law that forbid contacts with the PLO, that prohibit the PLO from opening an office in the United States, or that constrict providing aid to the PLO through the United Nations. (The Middle East Peace Facilitation Act of 1993, P.L. 103-125, October 28, 1993; amended and renewed several times, most recently in P.L. 104-107, February 12, 1996). The current MEPFA and the President's waiver authority expired on August 12, 1997. The most recent combined MEPFA-PLOCCA report to Congress appeared on January 12, 1997, covered both the PLO Commitment Compliance Act and the Middle East Peace Facilitation Act, and found that the PLO was complying with its commitments. The May 7, 2002 PLOCCA report does not include a determination that the PLO is complying with its commitments.

In May 1997, Members of Congress threatened to cut U.S. aid to the Palestinians because Palestinian leaders advocated applying a 1973 Jordanian law that called for the death penalty for Palestinians who sold land to Israelis or Jews. On June 10, 1997, the House passed by voice vote an amendment to H.R. 1757, the Foreign Relations Authorization bill, that called upon Palestinian leaders to renounce the death penalty, and stated that the President and Congress will consider Palestinian actions when considering renewal of the Middle East Peace Facilitation Act that expired on August 12, 1997. Other Members of Congress suggested cutting aid to the Palestinians because they believed that the PLO or the Palestinian Authority incited recent terror attacks against Israel. News reports that an internal PA audit released on May 25, 1997, disclosed corruption and waste prompted other Members of Congress to question U.S. aid to the Palestinians. After allowing the Middle East Peace Facilitation Act to expire on August 12, 1997, Congress added sections to the Foreign Operations Appropriations bill, H.R. 2159, that gave the President waiver authority similar to the MEPFA waivers. (See, for example, Sections 539(d), 552, and 566 of P.L. 105-118, November 26, 1997, and Sections 553, 556, and 566 of P.L. 105-277 of October 21, 1998, or Section 538(d) of H.R. 3194 of November 19, 1999.)

Section 584 of P.L. 105-277 of November 21, 1998, and Section 578 of H.R. 3194 of November 19, 1999, and Section 574 of P.L. 106-429 of November 6, 2000, prohibit any aid funds for the Palestine Broadcasting Corporation (PBC). The United States provided about $250,000 for training and equipment for the PBC in 1995 but withdrew the aid when it was feared that Arafat would use the public station for political purposes. The United States continues to help Palestinian journalists, but does not provide direct support to the PBC. The ban on aid to the PBC is continued in Section 561 of H.R. 5410, the Foreign Operations Appropriations bill for FY2003 in conference.

The House of Representatives passed H.Con.Res. 426 by a vote of 365 to 30 on October 25, 2000; the resolution expressed solidarity with Israel and condemned Palestinian Arab leaders for encouraging violence in the continuing confrontations that began following Likud Party leader Sharon's visit to the Haram al-Sharif/Temple Mount area of Jerusalem on September 28.

Eighty-seven U.S. Senators and 209 Representatives signed similar letters to President Bush on April 5, 2001, advising that Palestine President Arafat not be invited to the White House until the Intifadah ended, that the Palestinian leadership was responsible for orchestrating the Intifadah, and that the United States should stop aid to the Palestinians.

P.L. 107-115 (H.R. 2506), the foreign operations appropriations bill for FY2002 signed into law on January 10, 2002, requires the President to report to Congress on PLO compliance with past commitments. If not in compliance, the President may close the PLO office in Washington, designate the PLO constituents as terrorist groups, and/or limit humanitarian assistance to the Palestinians.

The House passed H.Res. 392 by a vote of 352-21 with 29 "present" on May 2, 2002. The bill states that the Palestinian leadership incites and supports terrorism against Israel. The Administration opposed the bill because it could hamper U.S. efforts to mediate an Israeli-Palestinian cease-fire. The bill vows U.S. solidarity with Israel and justifies Israel's use of force against the Palestinians. The Senate passed S.Amdt. 3389 to H.R. 3009, the Andean Trade bill, the same day, also justifying Israel's actions against the Palestinians.

H.R. 4693, introduced on May 9, 2002, finds that Arafat and the PLO are responsible for terrorism against Israelis, states that it is the sense of Congress that Arafat and the PLO should end support for terrorism, and imposes sanctions on the PLO and the PA.

Title VI of the Foreign Relations Authorization Act of 2002 (P.L. 107-228, H.R. 1646), entitled the Middle East Peace Commitments Act of 2002, repeats many aspects of PLOCCA, MEPFA, and the reporting requirements in the appropriations bills mentioned above. Section 604(c) provides for a presidential waiver of the Act's sanctions applicable to the Palestinians.

Palestinian Statehood

On November 15, 1988, the Palestine Liberation Organization National Council declared a Palestinian state with its capital in Jerusalem. Some 100 nations recognized the new state even though it did not have a government or any territory under its sovereignty. Despite the 1988 declaration, in February 1998, Palestinian leader Arafat said he would declare a state unilaterally on May 4, 1999, the date set in the 1994 Gaza-Jericho Agreement for completing the permanent status talks. Later Arafat delayed the declaration while Israel held its elections and during the negotiations that led up to the Wye and Sharm al-Shaykh agreements, but he later renewed his intention to declare the state, selecting September 13, 2000, the new date the two sides set for completing the permanent status negotiations. The PLO Central Council announced on September 10, 2000, that the declaration of statehood would be delayed pending the outcome of the current peace negotiations, but the declaration is further delayed by the Intifadah. Israeli leaders oppose the Palestinian declaration of statehood because they feel that the future status of the Palestinian entity should be a subject in the talks.

Several U.S. Administrations have decried unilateral actions that could interrupt the peace talks, and the Clinton Administration had cautioned Arafat not to declare a state unilaterally. H.Con.Res. 24, passed by the House on March 16, 1999, and the Senate on April 12, 1999, states that a unilateral declaration of Palestinian statehood would draw strong congressional opposition and that the President should assert that a statehood declaration would violate the Oslo accords. (Palestinian statehood is not mentioned in the Oslo agreements.) The House voted 385 to 27 (with four present) on September 27, 2000, to pass H.R. 5272, which would have cut off U.S. foreign assistance to the Palestinians if the Palestinians declared a state without Israeli agreement.

On September 24, 2001, President Bush said that a state of Palestine was part of the vision for a future resolution of the Arab-Israel problem. The statement was reinforced by other Administration spokesmen in the following months. U.N. Security Council Resolution 1397, passed by a vote of 14-0-1 (Syria) on March 12, 2002, included the phrase "two states, Israel; and Palestine," the first U.N. Security Council resolution to mention a Palestinian state. Observers noted that the United States sponsored the resolution and voted in favor.

Current Negotiations Between Israel and the Palestinians

As far as is known, there are no current negotiations between the Palestinians and Israelis.

The "quartet" peace plan (Europe, Russia, U.N., U.S.A.) remains under consideration but with no clear indication of if or when the plan would be implemented. During stage one of phase one, the Israelis will end attacks on Palestinian cities, end house demolitions, end deportations, and dismantle settlements established since February 2001, and the Palestinians will name a new cabinet (done on October 29, 2002), name a Prime Minister, end violence against Israelis, and consolidate the Palestinian police forces. During stage two of phase one, the IDF will withdraw to the September 28, 2000 lines and freeze all settlement activity. The Palestinians and the Israelis will sign a new security agreement. The Palestinians will hold elections for the Palestinian Legislative Council.

During Phase two, the quartet will establish a monitoring system to monitor compliance with the agreement and will hold an international conference on Palestinian economic recovery. The quartet also will sponsor negotiations for a Palestinian state within provisional borders. During phase three, scheduled to begin in 2004, Israel and the Palestinians will agree on a provisional Palestinian state and, by the beginning of 2005, will resume negotiations for permanent borders, Jerusalem, refugees, settlements, and other unresolved issues.

Unresolved Issues in the Palestine Problem

Jerusalem

Palestinians claim that Israel must withdraw from east Jerusalem, seized by Israel in the 1967 war along with the rest of the West Bank. Palestinians maintain that east Jerusalem will become the capital of the Palestinian state. Israel, which has claimed Jerusalem as its capitol since 1948, annexed east Jerusalem in 1967, and claims that Jerusalem's status is not negotiable. No other country recognizes Israel's annexation of east Jerusalem.

The July 25, 1994 Jordan-Israel non-belligerency agreement states that Israel "respects ... the special role" played by Jordan in Muslim religious shrines in Jerusalem. Arafat had stated in the past that the Palestinian entity would be responsible for non-Jewish religious shrines in the holy city. The Jordan-Israel agreement appears to set the stage for a future contest or cooperation between Jordan and Palestine over the religious sites.

The United States has maintained a policy since 1967 that the future of the city must be negotiated and cannot be decided unilaterally, and that the city should not be divided as it was between 1948 and 1967. In 1990, Congress opposed the Administration position and passed resolutions acknowledging that Jerusalem was the capital of Israel and should not be a divided city (H.Con.Res. 290, passed on April 24, 1990, and S.Con.Res. 106, passed on March 22, 1990). In 1995, Congress passed S. 1322 (P.L. 104-45, November 8, 1995) that stated that the U.S. embassy should be moved from Tel Aviv to Jerusalem. The law provides a presidential waiver if maintaining the embassy in Tel Aviv is in the U.S. national interest. On July 27, 2000, President Clinton told an Israeli interviewer that he favored moving the embassy to Jerusalem, but signed waivers to keep the embassy in Tel Aviv. During the 2000 campaign, George Bush said he favored moving the embassy to Jerusalem, but since becoming President has signed waivers delaying the move.

Section 214 of P.L. 107-228, the Foreign Relations Authorization Act for FY2003, states that Congress maintains its commitment to moving the U.S. embassy from Tel Aviv to Jerusalem, bans funds appropriated in the Act from being used to support the Jerusalem consulate unless the U.S. ambassador to Israel has authority over the consulate, declares that publications financed under the Act must list Jerusalem as the capital of Israel, and states that any U.S. citizen born in Jerusalem may request that their birthplace be listed as Israel. President Bush issued a statement on September 30, 2002, that he considered the section to be advisory, not binding, and that the section interfered with his constitutional authority to conduct the nations' foreign relations. The statement also said that U.S. policy toward Jerusalem remained unchanged, which implied that the United States holds that the future of Jerusalem must be negotiated and not be decided unilaterally, as the Israelis have done.

Boundaries

The Palestinians would prefer a return to the boundaries recommended by the United Nations in Resolution 181 of 1947, but since 1974, have accepted the 1948-1967 boundaries between the West Bank/Gaza and Israel. The Shamir government (1988- 1992) claimed all of the West Bank as part of Israel, and would have made the boundary the Jordan River. It is not clear what compromise the Rabin-Peres government (1992- 1996) would have offered or accepted.

The Palestinian-Israeli Interim Agreement, September 1995, partitioned the 2,200 square mile West Bank into a patchwork quilt composed of three different jurisdictions: Area A, under full Palestinian control, about 1% of the total, was comprised of the seven largest cities (excluding Jerusalem), primarily populated by Palestinian Arabs; Area B, under shared Palestinian and Israeli control, about 27% of the West Bank, was comprised of Arab villages around the cities; and Area C, under full Israeli control, about 72% of the total, was comprised of Israeli settlements, so-called "state land," highways, public areas, and Israeli military bases.

Israel withdrew from the Area A cities in December 1995-January 1996 (and Hebron February 1997) and a few of the Area B villages, leaving the Palestinian Authority in control of about 3% of the West Bank. Israel also withdrew from 70% of the Gaza Strip, but retained four areas where there are Jewish settlements. The Netanyahu government ceded another 7% of the West Bank in November 1998, in keeping with the Wye agreement, but postponed further withdrawals until after the May 1999 election. The government of Ehud Barak, sworn in July 1999, agreed in September 1999 to further withdrawals in September and November 1999, and March 2000, that left about 18% of the West Bank in Palestinian hands, 22% under shared Israeli-Palestinian control, and 60% under full Israeli control.

According to press reports in early May 2000, Israel offered to withdraw from a total of 80% of the West Bank, withdrawing from 66% now and the remaining 14% after a couple of years. Israel would annex the remaining 20%. The Palestinians rejected the offer. The press reported on May 20 that Israel raised the offer to 90% of the West Bank, and an unconfirmed rumor circulating in August 2000 said that the United States proposed that Israel retain only 5% of the West Bank. Reports from the July 2000 Camp David talks said the figures under discussion ranged from 90% to 97%. The Palestinians rejected the Israeli Camp David offer because Israel retained sovereignty over all of Jerusalem – the Palestinians sought sovereignty over Arab east Jerusalem – and because the Israeli proposal divided the West Bank into three non-contiguous zones that would have impaired Palestinian nationalism and stymied economic growth.

France and Saudi Arabia suggested in February 2002 that Israel exchange withdrawal from the occupied territories for Arab recognition of Israel. It is not clear if the Saudi and French proposals are for full withdrawal or if the extent of the Israeli withdrawal is negotiable.

Palestinians consider the Golan Heights part of Syria, not Palestine, but the Syrian-Israeli negotiations over the Golan may affect Palestinian-Israeli negotiations over the West Bank and Gaza. Persistent rumors from Israel and unconfirmed reports from Syria claim that the Rabin-Peres government agreed to withdraw from most of the Golan Heights. The Netanyahu government elected in May 1996, appeared less inclined to withdraw from Golan and not inclined to meet a commitment made by its predecessor government. Periodic unconfirmed rumors circulating in Israel suggest that Israeli-Syrian talks continue in secret.

The United States has stated that boundaries should be negotiated and mutually recognized, "should not reflect the weight of conquest," and that adjustments in the pre-1967 boundaries should be "insubstantial." The U.S. position acknowledges the Israeli need for defensible borders (erase some of the anomalies along the 1948-1967 armistice lines) and also acknowledges the Palestinian desire for a territorial entity separate from Israeli rule.

Israeli Settlements in the Occupied Territories

The Arab nations maintain that Israeli settlements in the occupied territories are illegal under international law, specifically paragraph 6 of Article 49 of the Fourth Geneva Convention on the Protection of Civilian Persons in Time of War, which states: "The occupying power shall not deport or transfer parts of its own civilian population into territories it occupies." Israel maintains that Jordan's 1950 annexation of the West Bank was not recognized by the international community, and therefore is illegal. Egypt never claimed the Gaza Strip. Israel maintains that the two regions are not "occupied territories," and are not subject to the Geneva Convention and rightfully belong to Israel. Many nations, as reflected in the votes on several U.N. General Assembly and Security Council resolutions, believe that Israel is the occupying power, that the Geneva Convention applies, and that the Israeli settlements are illegal. United States' spokesmen, such as Ambassador George Bush on September 25, 1971, Ambassador William Scranton on May 26, 1976, and Secretary of State Cyrus Vance on March 21, 1980, have stated that the settlements are illegal. During a December 16, 1996 news conference, President Bill Clinton agreed with the statement that the settlements were obstacles to peace. President George Bush said on April 4, 2002, that Israeli settlement activity in the occupied territories must stop.

Compensation/Repatriation for Palestinian Refugees

Palestinians argue that paragraph 11 of U.N.G.A. Resolution 194 of December 11, 1948, states that the Arab refugees have a choice between returning to the homes now in Israel that they left during the 1947-1948 war, or receiving compensation for the lost property. Israel argues that the Arabs abandoned their property voluntarily, and that the international community should provide funding for resettling the Palestinian refugees in Arab countries. Arabs claim the Jews drove them from their homes in 1948-1949. Some Israelis counter with a claim for compensation for property abandoned by Jews who left or were driven from Arab countries in the aftermath of the 1948-1949 war.

Israel claims that allowing Palestinian refugees to return to homes left in 1948-1949 or 1967 will destroy the Jewish nature of Israel. Palestinians claim the right of return is a matter of justice encased in international law. The argument may be one of perception rather than physically moving a number of Palestinians into Israel: by accepting the right of return, Israel may be accepting blame for forcing the refugees out of their homes in the first place, and the Palestinians may be more interested in such a confession of guilt than in the actual return to abandoned properties.

Demilitarized Zones and Peacekeeping Forces

In the past, both Arabs and Israelis have accepted demilitarized zones and peacekeeping forces stationed in the zones or along the borders, although Israel will not accept peacekeeping forces in its territory. Many believe the Palestinians will accept demilitarizing the West Bank/Gaza state they hope to form. Israel rejected a Palestinian suggestion that the Israeli Defense Forces withdraw from the occupied territories to be replaced by an international peacekeeping force to maintain order during the 5-year interim period, but Israel did accept Temporary International Presence in Hebron (TIPH) in 1994 (primarily composed of Danish, Norwegian, Swedish, Swiss, Italian, and Turkish police officers) to monitor the boundaries between the 120,000 Palestinians and 450 Israeli settlers living in Hebron. Arafat suggested, in September 1996, that the United States send a peacekeeping force to police Hebron, but the suggestion was dismissed immediately by Israel and the United States. TIPH announced it would pull out of Hebron on August 23, 2001, because of continuing harassment by the Israeli settlers. The United States vetoed a U.N. Security Council resolution on March 27, 2001, that would have created a U.N. observer force to monitor Israeli actions against Palestinians in the occupied territories but signed the G8 foreign ministers declaration on July 19 that endorsed monitors.

Palestinians and the Peace Process

The Palestine Liberation Organization and Palestinian Representation

The PLO was founded by the Arab League in 1964 (although some claim predecessor groups date back to the 1950s). The PLO is an umbrella organization composed of many constituent groups, the most prominent of which are the several military groups that have been involved in unconventional warfare against Israel. Other groups represented within the PLO are humanitarian agencies, welfare organizations, educational groups, medical institutions, professional organizations, women's groups, workers, and others. These groups are represented in the Palestine National Council (PNC), the 600+ member parliament, in the 90-member Central Council, which acts as a steering committee when the PNC is not in session, and the 18-member Executive Committee (four of whom resigned in opposition to the Declaration of Principles), which acts as a cabinet. The PLO is supported by taxes collected from Palestinian workers in Arab countries, from donations, from contributions from other Arab governments, and from profits of PLO business enterprises. Several Arab governments stopped their contributions to the PLO because of PLO support for Iraq's invasion of Kuwait in 1990.

In the past, Israeli leaders rejected the PLO as the Palestinian representative, claiming that the PLO is a terrorist organization committed to destroying Israel. On September 10, 1993, Prime Minister Rabin and Chairman Arafat exchanged letters granting mutual recognition.

Opposition

Not all Palestinians support the peace talks. A few Palestinians, primarily represented by groups headquartered in Damascus, prefer to maintain the state of war until Israel is defeated and the state of Israel is removed from the Middle East. Another group of Palestinians reject the September 1993 PLO-Israel agreement because it does not provide for an independent Palestinian state, does not call for an immediate and complete Israeli withdrawal from occupied territory, ties the Palestinian economy to Israel, and did not provide for immediate release of all Palestinian prisoners in Israeli jails. Among the groups opposing the peace process are the Popular Front for the Liberation of Palestine (PFLP), the Palestine Liberation Front (PLF), the PFLP-General Command (all in Damascus), and Hamas in the occupied territories. The Democratic Front for the Liberation of Palestine (DFLP) shifted to supporting the talks.

The Palestinian Entity

Government

On May 12, 1994, PLO Chairman Arafat named 15 members of a 24-person cabinet to govern the Gaza/Jericho enclaves. On May 24, 1994, Arafat canceled all Israeli laws and reinstated pre-1967 laws in Gaza and Jericho in an attempt to erase the Israeli occupation presence. Under terms of the September 13, 1993 Declaration of Principles, the Palestinian cabinet assumed responsibility for health, education and culture, social welfare, direct taxation, and tourism. The 88-

seat Palestinian Authority (also called the Palestinian Legislative Council or the Palestinian National Authority), elected on January 20, 1996, and sworn in on March 7, 1996, and the 26-person cabinet named by President Yasir Arafat on May 9, 1996, assumed responsibility over other functions of government except for security and foreign relations, which Israel controlled through the 5-year interim and into the final negotiating period. Arafat named a new 34-person cabinet on August 5, 1998, to avoid a vote of confidence in the Palestinian Legislative Council, and on June 13, 2002, reduced the cabinet to 21 members as part of his reform program. The cabinet resigned on September 19, 2002. Arafat called for municipal, PLC, and presidential elections in December 2002 or January 2003. The United States and others have proposed that the Palestinians name a prime minister as a way to sidestep Arafat's authority, but Arafat opposes the suggestion.

The PLC passed a Basic Law in 1997, but Arafat did not sign the law until May 30, 2002. The Basic Law serves as a constitution, outlining the function of the PLC, the President, the cabinet, and the electoral process.

Police

According to negotiations following the May 4, 1994 agreement, the Palestinian enclaves were to be protected by a Palestinian police force drawn from the Palestine Liberation Army (PLA) units stationed in Egypt, Jordan, and Iraq, and Palestinians recruited from the occupied territories, Jordan, Egypt, Yemen, Tunisia, and other Palestinian concentrations. The Palestinian police began arriving in Gaza on May 11 and in Jericho on May 12, 1994, replacing the Israeli Defense Forces and Israeli border police. Other nations have provided training (Egypt, Jordan, Great Britain, Iraq), vehicles (the United States donated 200 light and heavy trucks, Russia donated armored vehicles, Greece donated 58 trucks), uniforms (Norway), communications equipment (Spain), anti-riot gear (Great Britain), housing and offices (Japan and Germany), and cash (the United States $5 million, European Union). The Palestinian police are supposed to cooperate with the Israeli police in patrolling the borders and the villages, manning crossing points, and maintaining order. Paragraph 3 of Article IV of Annex I of the Interim Agreement of September 28, 1995, states that the Palestinian police force shall number 12,000 in the West Bank and 18,000 in the Gaza Strip. According to Palestinian reports, there are about 30,000 uniformed Palestinian police and another 3 to 4,000 clerical and support personnel. Israel claims that there are between 36,000, and 40,000 Palestinian police in uniform; some Israelis claim there are 50,000 police. Israel destroyed most of the Palestinian police infrastructure during the Israeli invasions of West Bank cities in April-May 2002.

Economy

Israel's closure of the occupied territories has forced the near collapse of the Palestinian economy. Israel has closed Palestinian borders with Egypt, Israel, and Jordan, and has cordoned off Palestinian towns and villages to prevent traffic between Palestinian areas. About 100,000 Palestinian workers cannot cross into Israel to jobs; the unemployment is at 50%, and gross domestic product has fallen by 50%. In its search for terrorist infrastructure, the IDF has destroyed much of the water, electrical, telephone, and transportation systems in Ramallah, Nablus, Jenin, and other West Bank cities. The Palestinian Authority relies upon grants from the Arab states and the European Union to meet its payroll.

Other Aspects of the Palestinians

Terrorism

Individual Palestinians and Palestinian military groups, both PLO and non-PLO, have launched terror attacks against Israeli people and facilities. Palestinian terrorists also have attacked people or institutions that, in the Palestinians view, support Israel, including U.S. citizens, property, and installations. One of the conditions set by Congress in 1984 for beginning a U.S. dialogue with the PLO was that the PLO renounce terrorism, which it did in November and December 1988. But when the PLO refused to renounce the May 30, 1990, attempted military landing near Tel Aviv, the United States broke off the dialogue. Israel maintained that the PLO is a terrorist group. Until January 1993, any contact between an Israeli or anyone under Israeli occupation and the PLO was a crime in Israel. Many Palestinians view the attacks against Israel and its supporters as part of the legitimate Palestinian armed struggle to secure Palestinian rights, and view Israeli attacks against Arab civilians as terrorism. On October 8, 1999, the Democratic Front for the Liberation of Palestine was removed from the State Department's terrorism list after the DFLP had agreed to rejoin the PLO and accept a peaceful resolution of the dispute with Israel.

Intifadah, 1987

In December 1987, an incident in the Gaza Strip touched off a continuing anti-Israeli civil uprising throughout the occupied territories that left about 1,900 Palestinians and almost 400 Israelis dead through April 1996. Some claim the Intifadah succeeded because the uprising compelled Israel to join the Madrid peace talks in October 1991. Others disagree, claiming Israel joined the Madrid talks at the insistence of the United States.

Palestine Refugees and UNRWA

One-half of the world's almost 8 million Palestinians live in Israel or under Israeli occupation. About 1 million Palestinian Arabs live in Israel and are Israeli citizens, who may vote and are eligible to serve in the Knesset (11 Arabs were elected to the Knesset in May 1996). The 3 million Palestinians in the occupied territories are not Israeli citizens and do not vote in Israeli elections. Jordan granted citizenship to the Palestinians living in Jordan but other Arab states have not offered blanket citizenship.

Of the 8 million Palestinians, 3.7 million are registered with the United Nations Relief and Works Agency (UNRWA) as refugees from the 1947-1948 war. There is disagreement over why the Palestinians became refugees: Israeli sources claim the Palestinians left their homes voluntarily or because the Arab governments told them to leave; Arab sources claim the Israelis forced the Palestinians to leave. UNRWA provides shelter, food, medical and dental care, and education benefits for the 3.7 million Palestinian refugees from the 1947-1948 war. Not all the registered refugees receive all the benefits; only 1.2 million live in 59 refugee camps scattered across Lebanon, Syria, Jordan, the West Bank, and the Gaza Strip.

Table 1. Palestine Arab Refugees Registered with UNRWA

Countries	1950 Total Registered	2000 Total Registered	No. of Camps	No. in Camps
Lebanon	127,600	376,472	12	210,715
Syria	82,194	383,199	10	111,712
Jordan	506,200	1,570,192	10	280,191
West Bank	—	583,009	19	157,676
Gaza Strip	198,227	824,622	8	451,186
Israel	45,800	—	—	—
Total	**960,021**	**3,737,494**	**59**	**1,211,480**

Source: Report of the Commissioner-General for UNRWA, Supplement 13 (A/55/13) 2000.

Note: West Bank included in Jordan in 1950. UNRWA stopped operating in Israel in 1952, when Israel resettled its Arab refugees.

The United States contributes to UNRWA through the refugee and migration account, authorized in the State Department authorization bill and appropriated through the foreign operations appropriations bill. U.S. contributions to UNRWA have not been earmarked in past appropriations bills.

Table 2. U.S. Contributions to UNRWA, 1950-2002
(millions of dollars)

Year	Amount
Cumulative 1950-1991	1,618
1992	69
1993	68
1994	78
1995	74
1996	77
1997	79
1998	78
1999	81
2000	89
2001	101
2002	100
Cumulative 1950-2002	2,514

Table 3. World Population of Palestinians, 1998

Jordan	2,328,308
West Bank (Israeli occupation)	1,596,554
Israel	953,497
Gaza Strip (Israeli occupation)	1,004,498
Lebanon	430,183
Kuwait	37,696
The Americas	203,588
Syria	465,662
Saudi Arabia	274,762
Egypt	48,784
Other Persian Gulf States	105,578
Iraq, Libya	74,284
All Other	264,792
Total	7,788,186

Source: Miftah.

Table 4. USAID Assistance to West Bank & Gaza, FY1975-FY2000
($ in thousands)

Fiscal Year	Actual/Est. Obligations
1975	$ 1,000
1976	1,572
1977	3,416
1978	2,687
1979	6,801
1980	3,000
1981	2,500
1982	6,000
1983	6,500
1984	8,500
1985	12,141
1986	13,950
1987	8,400
1988	6,911
1989	20,903
1990	12,618
1991	7,663
1992	7,074
1993	29,557
1994	56,769
1995	80,263
1996	64,306
1997	68,679
1998	60,685
1999	79,592
2000 (est.)	118,642
2001 (est.)	84,707
Total	$774,836

Chapter 2

HAMAS AND PALESTINIAN ISLAMIC JIHAD

Clyde Mark and Kenneth Katzman

INTRODUCTION

The recent activities of the radical Palestinian Islamist groups known as Hamas and Palestinian Islamic Jihad pose problems for the Palestinian self-governing authorities, Israel, and the U.S.-sponsored Arab-Israeli peace process. Despite April 1994 statements by some Hamas leaders that Hamas might join the Palestinian governing authority, the radical Islamist organizations have not accepted the concept that Israelis and Palestinians can share the territories of what was formerly Palestine. Hamas and Palestinian Islamic Jihad, as well as their supporters, see the Palestine Liberation Organization as having sold out the Palestinian people to Israel and its main ally, the United States.

Hamas and Palestinian Islamic Jihad have a core of guerrilla fighters who are willing and able to carry out military operations against their Palestinian enemies and Israel. According to Israeli sources, the Hamas guerrilla force numbers fewer than 100 at any given time, yet, in October 1994, Hamas carried its campaign into the heart of Israel, detonating a bomb aboard a passenger bus on Tel Aviv's main thoroughfare. Both radical Islamic groups, more so Hamas than Palestinian Islamic Jihad, also have substantial popular support among Palestinians in the West Bank and Gaza Strip. Some of that political support comes as a result of the charity work and social services that Hamas provides for its Palestinian constituents.

Hamas and Palestinian Islamic Jihad rely to some degree on outside support to sustain their operations, although the exact level of such support is not known. Iran, which shares the opposition of these groups to the peace process, is widely believed to be their main external sponsor. Along with its ally in Lebanon, Hizballah, Iran reportedly is providing not only funds but also training for Hamas and Palestinian Islamic Jihad fighters. However, the Palestinian Islamic groups also are funded by wealthy private contributors in the Persian Gulf states and from contributions raised from sympathizers in the United States and Europe. Syria and Jordan reportedly allow the groups to maintain a presence in their countries, but do not appear to fund them to any great extent.

In Israel and within the Palestinian governing authority, there is a debate over whether to crack down on the radical Islamic groups or to try to coopt them into joining the peace process. Those arguing for harsh measures believe there are no "moderate" elements in these groups with which to deal. Opponents contend that repression will only increase support for the radical Islamic Palestinian groups. The Clinton Administration and some in Congress are focussing on ways to deny outside support to the radical groups. Administration officials have said they might seek — and some in Congress want — legislation to bar private U.S. funds for Hamas and fundraising visits to this country by pro-Hamas leaders. The United States is also seeking to persuade its allies to restrict private support for the radical Palestinians. The Administration might have difficulty in stopping Iran from aiding the radical Palestinians because the United States has no political dialogue with Iran and it already has broad economic sanctions in force against that country.

BACKGROUND[1]

On December 8, 1987, a traffic accident at the Gaza Strip-Israel crossing point resulted in the deaths of several Palestinian Arabs, and triggered a series of increasingly violent demonstrations aimed at revenge against the Israeli occupying forces. Over the next few days, the rebellion, or "intifadah" in Arabic, spread to the West Bank, and eventually to some Arab areas of Israel, The Muslim Brotherhood, a branch of the Islamic reform movement founded in Egypt in 1928 and transplanted to Jerusalem in 1945, wanted to participate in the uprising, but feared damaging its non-political image as a religious, educational, and social

[1] For additional background, see: Wootten, James. Hamas: the Organization, Goals, and Tactics of a Militant Palestinian Organization. CRS Report to the Congress 93-511F, 19 August 1993.

organization. To avoid the military-political connection, several Muslim Brotherhood leaders, Shaykh Ahmad Yasin and Mahmud Zahhar among them, formed the Islamic Resistance Movement, Harakat al-Muqawama al-Islamiyya in Arabic (since known by its Arabic acronym Hamas, which also is the Arabic word for zeal).[2] Hamas issued leaflets in December 1987, encouraging continued participation in the uprising against the Israeli occupation but without using the Muslim Brotherhood or Hamas names. In February 1988, Hamas began using its name on leaflets and communiques, and identified itself as a militant branch of the Muslim Brotherhood. The Hamas Charter, adopted on 18 August 1988, states in Chapter One, Article 2, that Hamas is a branch of the Muslim Brotherhood.[3] But more recently, Hamas leaders rarely equate Hamas with the Muslim Brotherhood.

In the early 1980's, a group of Muslim Brotherhood members, led by Dr. Fathi al-Shaqaqi and Abd al-Aziz Audah, dissatisfied with the Brotherhoods' reluctance to confront Israel, formed the Islamic Jihad for Palestine. Islamic Jihad called for the removal of Israel through armed warfare, and the establishment of an Islamic state of Palestine. The Islamic Jihad maintains its militant opposition to Israel and to a negotiated agreement that recognizes two states in Palestine. During the same period, the 1980's, some members of Fatah, dissatisfied with the secular nature of the mainstream resistance movement, sought a more activist Islamic foundation for their attacks on Israel. Some of these dissatisfied Fatah members, depending on the degree of their commitment to Islam, joined Islamic Jihad or formed the more secular "Fatah Hawks." Both Islamic Jihad and the Fatah Hawks joined in the December 1987 intifadah.

Other Palestinian organizations, such as Fatah, the Popular Front for the Liberation of Palestine, or the Palestine Liberation Organization, were caught off guard by the sudden popularity of the spontaneous and spreading rebellion, and quickly began to organize support for the growing numbers of young Palestinians in the street and their families sequestered by Israeli curfews. The PLO and affiliated groups formed the Unified National Leadership of the Uprising (UNLU) to coordinate secular Palestinian support for the intifadah.[4] Militant Islamic groups, including Palestinian Islamic Jihad and Hamas, joined Fatah and other groups, both secular and religious, in forming a loose confederation called the

[2] Some observers believe Hamas was formed earlier: see for example Ahmad J. Rashad, Hamas: the History of the Islamic Opposition Movement in Palestine, Washington Report on Middle Eastern Affairs, vol. XI, no. 8, March 1993: 37-38.

[3] See Journal of Palestine Studies, vol. XXII, no. 4, Summer 1993: 122-134.

[4] Abu-Amr, Ziad. Hamas: a Historical and Political Background. Journal of Palestine Studies, vol. XXH, no. 4, Summer 1993: 5-19.

Unified National Command (UNC) to coordinate operations and support for those participating in the intifadah.[5]

STRUCTURE

Hamas follows, in general, an organizational structure similar to its parent Muslim Brotherhood. The general membership, which may number in the tens of thousands, is divided into areas, which are subdivided into sectors, which in turn are subdivided into regions and branches. Hamas has separate units for administration, intelligence, information, political affairs, and commando operations. Only the political and information units operate openly outside the occupied territories, maintaining offices in Amman, Damascus, Teheran, and other capitals. There is a Director-General to administer the day-to-day operations, and a Majlis al-Shura (advisory council) to set policy and advise on operations.

According to one Israeli source, the Hamas structure underwent some changes after Israel deported 415 Hamas leaders in December 1992,[6] Following the December 1992 kidnapping and murder of an Israeli policeman, Israel arrested some 1,000 Hamas and Islamic Jihad supporters. Israel deported 415 of the Islamists to Lebanon on 16/17 December 1992. The deportee case became the focus of international attention because the deportees languished on the slopes of southern Lebanon's hills through the winter and summer of 1993 before being repatriated to Israel and the occupied territories in December 1993. The Israeli arrests and deportations forced Hamas to reorganize and promote new leaders while the old Hamas leaders were detained in Lebanon, The Israeli sources also claimed that the Hamas military wing was all but destroyed at the time of the December 1992 deportations.

The military commando wing of Hamas is known as the Izz al-Din al-Qassim Brigades, named after a Palestinian nationalist killed fighting the British in the early 1930's, and probably numbers around 100 members at any given time.[7] Hamas military activities appeal to many Palestinians who want to confront the

---

[5] Some observers say there was only one organization and do not distinguish between the UNC and the UNLU.

[6] Yaari, Ehud. The Metamorphosis of Hamas. The Jerusalem Report, 14 January 1993: 24-26; Also see the interview with Ehud Yaari by Roni Daniyel, broadcast over Qol Israel (Voice of Israel) radio, 31 January 1993, printed in Foreign Broadcast Information Service, 31 January 1993.

[7] One Israeli source states that the number of Izz al-Din al-Qassim members is between 40 and 50, organized into 5 or 6 operational squads or cells. Horovitz, David and Ehud Yaari. Can Hamas Blow Up the Peace Process? The Jerusalem Report, Nov. 17,1994: 20-24.

Israeli occupiers, but at a continuing cost of constant Israeli military engagement and a growing cost of confrontations with the Palestinian police.

THE ISLAMIST PROGRAM

Hamas and Islamic Jihad assert that the area of the West Bank, the Gaza Strip, and Israel is a Muslim trust and should be a single Islamic state; that to accept any compromise solution that allows Israel to exist is a violation of the Muslim trust; that the Muslim Palestinian state to be formed will tolerate Jews and Christians among its citizens; and that Sharia (Islamic law) should be the law of the land in the Palestinian state. Hamas and Palestine Islamic Jihad use armed force against Israel in their attempt to create a Palestinian state. Hamas provides food, medical treatment and supplies, and education to the Palestinian Arabs of Gaza and the West Bank.

Recent Developments

In April 1994, Hamas spokesmen offered what appeared to be a modified policy. Khalid al-Hindi, dean of the Islamic University in Gaza and reportedly a Hamas leader, said on 21 April 1994 that Hamas would have accepted the 13 September 1993 Declaration of Principles if it had included full Israeli withdrawal from the West Bank and the Gaza Strip, and a dismantling of all Israeli settlements. A leaflet issued by the Izz al-Din al-Qassim group the same day, 21 April 1994, said the Hamas military wing would stop fighting the Israelis when Israel withdrew from the occupied territories. Also on 21 April, Hamas leader Musa Abu Marzuk was quoted as saying that Hamas would accept a truce if Israel withdrew from the West Bank, including east Jerusalem, and Gaza, if Israel dismantled all its settlements and evacuated all settlers, and if free elections were held in the territories.[8]

The change of policy, if indeed it was a change, followed three incidents that contradicted peace overtures, and appeared to fit a Hamas vow to revenge five-

---

[8] The al-Hindi statement appeared in an interview published in the Jerusalem Arabic newspaper al-Nahar, the Izz al-Din al-Qassim leaflet was reported in the Hebrew language newspaper al-Hamishmar, and the Abu Marzuk statement was broadcast over Monte Carlo radio; all three are reported in Foreign Broadcast Information Service, Daily Report on the Near East and South Asia, 22 April 1994. Not all Hamas sources agreed with the apparent shift in policy; al-Quds clandestine radio reported on 21 April that the "jihad" and military operations against Israel

fold the February 1994 incident at Hebron, in which an Israeli settler killed some 30 Palestinians. Hamas was implicated in the car bomb explosion that killed 8 and wounded 50 Israelis on a bus at Afula on 6 April, the explosion that killed 6 and wounded 25 on a bus at Hadera on 13 April, and the ax attack against Israelis in a Jerusalem bus on 18 April.[9]

ISLAMIST RELATIONS WITH OTHER PALESTINIAN GROUPS

The Islamist groups and the PLO agree on the need for a Palestinian state, but do not agree on all particulars about the hoped-for nation. The PLO wants the Palestinian state to be secular, not governed according to Sharia as advocated by the Palestinian Islamist groups. The PLO accepted and the Islamist groups rejected a two-state solution to the Arab-Israeli problem (sharing the territory between an Israeli state and an Arab state). The Muslim Brotherhood differs from some other Islamist groups and from the PLO in that it pursues a non-military path to Palestinian statehood.

The December 1992 deportations triggered a meeting between Hamas and the PLO that temporarily ended the near open warfare between the two groups, but the truce did not last.[10] Tensions between the radical Islamist groups and the PLO remain high and clashes between Hamas and the Palestinian police continue because of differences over the secular-religious nature of the Palestinian state they hope to form, control of areas and facilities, competition for members, and cooperation with the Israelis. The most recent incident, on 18 November 1994, began when the Palestinian police seized loudspeakers that Hamas members set up for a rally following Friday prayers. Hamas members responded with stones, and the police responded with gunfire. Fourteen died and 150 were wounded in the confrontation. In the days after the Friday clash, Arafat used the Fatah Hawks as irregular police to keep order, perhaps in an effort to lower the Palestinian police profile. Hamas claims that the Palestinian police, under direction of Arafat and the PLO, were cooperating with the Israeli authorities by arresting and detaining Hamas and Islamic Jihad members accused of attacking Israelis during October 1994.

---

would continue until Israel no longer occupied the Palestinian homeland; also reported in FBIS, 22 April 1994.

[9] All reported in FBIS, on 6 April 1994, 13 April 1994, and 18 April 1992.

[10] Kershner, Isabel. Hope and Fear. The Jerusalem Report, 14 January 1993; 27-29.

ISRAEL AND ISLAMIST GROUPS

Israel considers Hamas and Palestinian Islamic Jihad illegal terrorist organizations. Israel expects the Palestinian police, who began operating in Jericho and the Gaza Strip in May 1994, to pursue Islamist or other terrorists who attack Israelis in Israel or the occupied territories.

The Muslim Brotherhood, prior to 1987, limited its activity to religious and welfare issues, and did not engage in military or political confrontations with the Israeli occupation forces. Israel tolerated the non-threatening, service oriented Brotherhood. Hamas, with its more militant approach and its commando unit, was a threat to Israeli troops and settlers, and drew Israeli attention and enmity. But, there is some evidence that prior to intifadah or in the early days of Hamas formation, late 1987-early 1988, the Israeli government offered Hamas the same tolerance that it had offered to the Muslim Brotherhood, hoping that the Islamists would provide a counter to Fatah and the PLO.[11] After it became clear that Hamas was a more active political organization and that the military unit was acting against the Israeli occupying forces and Palestinian Arab collaborators, the Israeli support ended, and Israeli forces began attacking Hamas and its military wing. Israel used the same tactics against Hamas as it used against other Palestinians: detention, arrest, imprisonment, deporting known leaders, destroying houses and crops of activists' families, and, in some cases according to some evidence, harsh physical treatment.[12]

SUPPORT FOR THE PALESTINIAN ISLAMIST GROUPS

Hamas and Palestinian Islamic Jihad derive financial and political support from a wide range of sources, both from supporters in the West Bank and Gaza Strip and from countries and supporters in and outside the region. The financial aid takes many forms, ranging from small private contributions raised in mosques to large grants from wealthy contributors and some governments in the region.

[11] See Wilkinson, Paul. Hamas: an Assessment. Jane's Intelligence Review. July 1993: 313-314, Hamas and Friends. Economist, vol. 331, 23 April 1994:43.

[12] U.S. Congress. House of Representatives. Committee on Foreign Affairs, and Senate. Committee on Foreign Relations. Country Reports on Human Rights Practices for 1993. Submitted by the Department of State. 103rd Congress, 2nd session, Joint Committee Print. Washington, U.S.' Gov't. Print. Off., February 1994, pgs. 1203-1205.

Israeli sources reportedly estimate Hamas' total annual budget to be about $30 million.[13]

Local Support

The radical Palestinian Islamist groups appear to attract significant popular followings in their home bases in the West Bank and Gaza Strip. However, it is difficult to gauge precisely this support, in part because it fluctuates with the ebbs and flows of the peace process. At times when progress in the peace process has been slow, Hamas has often drawn as much as 35 to 45 percent of the vote in races for positions in local professional associations, unions, chambers of commerce, and student councils.[14] However, its underlying base of support throughout the West Bank and Gaza may be somewhat lower than that. A recent poll by the Center for Palestine Research and Studies reported in November 1994 that 17.4% of Palestinians in the West Bank and Gaza Strip claim political affiliation with Hamas, and 3.7% with Palestinian Islamic Jihad.[15]

Many Palestinians of all social classes are attracted to the Palestinian Islamist groups' ideological opposition to territorial compromise with Israel. Others, particularly the lower classes, are attracted to the Islamist groups for their ability to deliver social services (schools, medical clinics, sports clubs, religious community centers, food and money for orphans and poor families) that the Palestinian national authority or Israeli administration do not provide. This may explain why the Islamist groups are more popular in the poorer Gaza Strip than in the more affluent West Bank. Many supporters of the Palestinian Islamist groups provide funds in the form of contributions or levies; Hamas reportedly imposes a religious tax (zakat) of 2.5 percent on the wages of its members in the territories, but allegedly it sometimes uses threats of violence to compel payment.[16] Some observers contend that support for the radical Palestinian Islamic groups could drop if and when self-rule successfully is extended throughout the occupied territories and if the Palestinian Authority is able to accelerate economic development in the areas under its control.

---

[13] Ibrahim, Youssef. Palestinian Religious Militants: Why Their Ranks Are Growing. New York Times, November 8,1994. p A12.

[14] Greenberg, Joel. Self-Rule Pact Is Major Challenge to Islamic Militant Group in Gaza. New York Times, November 7,1993. p.10.

[15] The poll was conducted by the Nablus-based Center for Palestine Research and Studies during November 17-19. The poll was sponsored and published by the International Republican Institute: Washington, B.C. November 30, 1994.

[16] Wilkinson, Paul. Hamas-An Assessment. Jane's Intelligence Review, July 1993. p. 313.

The radical Palestinian Islamist groups' militia arms have a core of zealous, committed volunteers to carry out violent operations against their Palestinian enemies and against Israeli soldiers and civilians. The State Department estimates the strength of Hamas as an "unknown number of hardcore members, and tens of thousands of supporters and sympathizers," but says the strength of Palestinian Islamic Jihad is "unknown."[17] Israeli and Palestinian security authorities reportedly believe that Hamas' militia (the Izz al-Din al-Qassim Brigades) numbers fewer than 100 at any given time.[18] Hamas and Palestinian Islamic Jihad militiamen are drawn from overpopulated, impoverished neighborhoods that support the radical Palestinian Islamic groups and offer protection from Israeli and Palestinian security authorities. According to John Cooley, a well-known observer of Islamic movements, some of these militiamen served as volunteers in the war against Soviet forces in Afghanistan, as did many Islamic guerrillas now fighting secular regimes in Algeria, Egypt, and other countries.[19]

External Support

The October 11,1994 kidnapping of an Israeli soldier and the October 19, 1994 bombing of a Tel Aviv bus - for which Hamas claimed responsibility ~ have focussed greater attention on the external sponsorship of Hamas and Palestinian Islamic Jihad. In some cases, the Palestinian Islamist groups receive outside financial aid from private contributors, although in other cases the groups may receive aid directly from sympathetic governments in the region. Some regional governments may be acting as unwitting or reluctant hosts for efforts by Iran to provide assistance to its Islamist Palestinian allies.

Iran

Iran, Hamas, and Palestinian Islamic Jihad all oppose compromise with Israel, and Iran is the most vocal governmental sponsor of the radical Palestinian Islamic groups. Iran argues that territorial compromise with Israel by the Palestine Liberation Organization (PLO) and its Palestinian allies represents a sellout of Muslim rights. For the most part, Iranian leaders have been open about their support for Hamas and Palestinian Islamic Jihad, and these groups, especially

[17] U.S. Department of State. Office of the Coordinator for Counterterrorism. Patterns of Global Terrorism: 1993. Released April 1994. pp. 45, 56.

[18] Ibrahim, Youssef. Palestinian Religious Militants: Why Their Ranks Are Growing. New York Times, November 8,1994. pA12.

[19] *Presentation by John* Cooley at a Middle East Institute sponsored briefing for congressional staff. November 18, 1994.

Palestinian Islamic Jihad, similarly have been public in acknowledging their affinity for Iran. During a visit to the United Nations in New York in April 1994, Iran's Foreign Minister Velayati said Iran would continue to provide "political and emotional" support for Palestinian groups that rejected the September 1993 Israel-PLO Declaration of Principles on Interim Self-Government, though he denied Iran provided military aid to those groups. Since the accord, several Iranian officials, including the Commander-in-Chief of Iran's Revolutionary Guard, have met with Hamas and Palestinian Islamic Jihad leaders in Damascus, lauding these organizations and their goals.[20] There have been press reports that the Revolutionary Guard is training Hamas and Palestinian Islamic Jihad activists in Lebanon (where the Guard maintains a contingent of troops) and in Sudan, where Revolutionary Guards reportedly also are present.[21] It should be noted that hard evidence of Iranian military training of Palestinian Islamic militants is lacking. For their part, Hamas leaders have said that Hamas and Iran share an "identical view in the strategic outlook towards the Palestinian cause in its Islamic dimension,"[22] and Palestinian Islamic Jihad leaders have acknowledged Iranian political support.

It is increasingly clear that Iran provides funding to the Islamic Palestinian groups, although the funding levels are not precisely known. In the aftermath of the Tel Aviv bus bombing, Israel's Ambassador to the United States, Itamar Rabinovich, said "I think that speaking in state or government terms, Iran is the address [the main source of external funding for Hamas]."[23] The State Department's Office of Counter-terrorism supports the Israeli allegations of Iranian funding, noting in its report on international terrorism for 1993 that Hamas and Palestinian Islamic Jihad receive funding from Iran.[24] On the other hand, some dispute the implication that acceptance of Iranian funding means that Iran somehow controls the radical Palestinian Islamist movements or that it drives actions these groups commit. Hamas receives funding from a wide range of sources, and it is not necessarily beholden to Iran as a sole benefactor. Some analysts of Iranian affairs have noted that, despite its rhetoric, the clerical regime

---

[20] Iranian Official Discusses Ways to Foil Peace Pact. Reuters, November 17, 1993. Hamas and Palestinian Islamic Jihad are part of a ten member, Damascus-based front of Palestinian rejectionist groups, which includes some extreme nationalist and leftist Palestinian organizations.

[21] Horowitz, David, with Ya'ari, Ehud. Can Hamas Blow Up the Peace Process? Jerusalem Report, November 17,1994. pp. 23-4.

[22] Hamas Says It Sees Iran as Strategic Ally. Reuters, February 28, 1993.

[23] Itamar Rabinovich Press Conference, Washington, D.C. Reuters, October 19, 1994.

[24] U.S. Department of State. Office of the Coordinator for Counterterrorism. Patterns of Global Terrorism: 1993. Released April 1994. pp. 45-6, 56.

has taken, as far as is known, little direct action to derail the peace process,[25] and that sectarian differences between the Sunni Muslim Palestinian groups and Shiite Muslim Iran limit their potential to remain allies.

The Israeli and U.S. assessments have been confirmed indirectly by some Palestinian Islamic leaders, including Fathi al-Shaqaqi, the Secretary General of Palestinian Islamic Jihad. In April 1993, he told a New York newspaper that Palestinian Islamic Jihad has received Iranian funds since 1987 and that "Hamas and four other groups are likewise funded by Tehran."[26] Hamas' representative in Iran said in 1993 that "there were forms of assistance from the Iranian people to help the steadfastness of the Palestinian people in the occupied territories," but he denied that Hamas had received as much as $30 million from Iran, as alleged by PLO leader Yasir Arafat.[27] A Lebanese newspaper that often has proved reliable on Iranian affairs reported in December 1993 that Hamas, as of January 1994, would receive $10 million (presumably per year) from Iran, to be derived from spot sales of Iranian oil stored in Rotterdam, the Netherlands.[28]

Lebanon/Hizballah

Following fifteen years of civil war, the government of Lebanon is trying, with mixed success, to extend its control throughout Lebanon, but Israeli, Syrian, and Iranian forces and their local allies continue to maintain a presence in Lebanon. The most important militia operating in Lebanon is the radical Shiite Islamic Hizballah organization, a close ally of Iran, and there appear to be growing links between Hizballah and the radical Palestinian Islamist groups.[29] Hizballah and the Palestinian Islamic groups have organized demonstrations in Beirut denouncing the September 13,1993 Israel-PLO accord and the October 26,1994 peace treaty between Jordan and Israel. When Israel returned the last of the 415 Hamas and Palestinian Islamic Jihad deportees in December 1993, Hizballah and Iranian Revolutionary Guard officials helped the deportees dismantle their tent camps in the no-man's land between Israel and Lebanon.[30] As further evidence of the growing bonds between the Palestinian Islamic groups and

---

[25] Amirahmadi, Hooshang. The Islamic Republic and the Question of Palestine. Middle East Insight, May-August 1994. pp. 50-54.

[26] Jihad Leader Acknowledges Iranian Funding. London Al Sharq Al Awsat, quoting Shaqaqi's interview with New York Newsday. April 12, 1993. p.4.

[27] Hamas Says It Sees Iran as Strategic Ally. Reuters, February 28, 1993.

[28] $10 Million Reportedly Granted to Hamas. Beirut Al-Shira,' December 1993, p.9.

[29] For further information on Hizballah, see U.S. Library of Congress. Congressional Research Service. Hizballah: A Radical Militia in Lebanon. CRS Report 93-905 F, October 7,1993, by Kenneth Katzman.

[30] Hoffman, David. Palestinian Militants' Exile in Lebanon Ends. Washington Post, December 16,1993. p. A35.

Hizballah, the Hamas militants who kidnapped Israeli soldier Nachshon Waxman in October 1994 demanded the release not only of Palestinian Islamic leaders, but also of Hizballah leaders kidnapped by Israel (Shaykh Abd al-Karim Ubayd and Mustafa Dirani).[31] There are some unconfirmed reports that Hizballah, along with Iranian Revolutionary Guards based in Lebanon, is training Hamas (and presumably also Palestinian Islamic Jihad) fighters in Lebanon.[32]

Syria

According to the State Department, Syria may be providing some funds to Palestinian Islamic Jihad.[33] There are no official U.S. allegations of Syrian funding for Hamas, but some Members of Congress have alleged that there is Syrian support for Hamas. The Secretary-General of Palestinian Islamic Jihad, Fathi al-Shaqaqi, is based in Damascus and Syria allows Hamas and Palestinian Islamic Jihad representatives -- along with eight of their anti-peace Palestinian allies - to operate in Damascus as a rejectionist front. Syria probably hosts -these groups, at least in part, as potential leverage in negotiations with Israel, and as a means of preserving Syria's alliance with Iran, from which Syria reportedly gets some oil and political support. Perhaps more significant is Syria's tacit approval of cooperation between the Palestinian Islamic groups and Hizballah and Iran in Lebanon. Hizballah and Iran's Revolutionary Guard operate in Lebanon in areas, such as the Bekaa Valley, that are under the direct control of Syria's approximately 35,000 troops in Lebanon. On the other hand, Syria has often acted to rein in Hizballah or other groups when their clashes with Israel have escalated to the point at which the Arab-Israeli peace process is in jeopardy. Syria is believed willing to expel Hizballah's militia, Iranian forces, and radical Palestinian elements from Lebanon in conjunction with a peace settlement with Israel that leads to a full return of the Golan Heights to Syria and an Israeli withdrawal from southern Lebanon.

Jordan

Until recently, Jordan had tacitly supported the Muslim Brotherhood in the West Bank and, through it, Hamas, believing that building up Hamas would help weaken the influence of the PLO in the West Bank. (The PLO and Jordan have vied for support among Palestinians in the West Bank.) Jordan has aided Hamas

---

[31] Gellman, Barton. Hamas Kidnaps Israeli, Threatens to Kill Him. Washington Post, October 12, 1994. p.A27.

[32] Background on Hamas, in Middle East Week. Center for Near East Research. December 29,1992. p.5.

[33] Patterns of Global Terrorism: 1993. p.56.

through Jordan's Islamic endowments ministry, which maintains mosques and funds Islamic clerics in the West Bank.[34] In the last few years, however, Jordan increasingly has become concerned that Hamas' militancy might radicalize its sister organization in Jordan, the Muslim Brotherhood, which is now a key bloc in the Jordanian parliament. In April 1994, reportedly with some U.S. urging, King Hussein declared Hamas illegal in Jordan.[35]

There is some circumstantial evidence to suggest that Jordan unwittingly or reluctantly is hosting a potential Iranian conduit to Hamas. Iran has no presence in the West Bank or Gaza Strip, where Hamas operates, but, in 1992, Iran reopened its embassy in Jordan, from which Hamas activists can gain relatively easy access to the West Bank. In 1993, Iran appointed Ahmad Dastmalchian as its Ambassador to Jordan. Dastmalchian had served during 1987-1990 in Lebanon where he helped funnel Iranian assistance to Hizballah; Jordan reportedly had hesitated to accept his appointment in Amman because of concerns that he would seek to back Islamic extremists in Jordan.[36] In January 1994, Jordan demanded Iran cut its embassy staff in Amman from forty persons to nine; Dastraalchian remained in place.[37] That month, King Husayn said that Dastmalchian was "acting as an Ambassador should," but that Jordan was watching the Iranian embassy closely.[38] Based on Dastmalchian's background and the circumstances of his appointment in Amman, it is possible that he might aid Hamas through Iran's embassy there, if assertions of Iranian aid to Hamas are true.

Persian Gulf States - Private Contributors

The State Department believes that Hamas is receiving some funding from private contributors in Saudi Arabia and other moderate Arab states.[39] Saudi Arabia is a conservative Islamic state that has supported Islamic movements throughout the Middle East. In addition, Saudi Arabia and the other Persian Gulf states were angered by the PLO's support of Iraq during the 1990-91 Gulf crisis, and have backed the radical Palestinian groups as an expression of their displeasure with the PLO. Exact estimates of aid from Gulf state contributors are difficult to obtain, but one report, quoting Western intelligence sources, says Hamas gets "millions" of dollars annually from private contributors in the Gulf

[34] Bailey, Clinton. Hamas: The Fundamentalist Challenge to the PLO. Washington, D.C.: Washington Institute for Near East Policy. Research Memorandum Number 19, April 1992. pp. 16 -17.
[35] Sabbagh, Rana. Jordan Says Hamas Is Illegal. Reuters, April 16, 1994.
[36] Sabbagh, Rana. Jordan Tells Iran to Reduce Diplomats in Amman. Reuters, January 22,1994.
[37] Iran to Cut Staff at Amman Embassy by 31. Reuters, February 5, 1994.
[38] Boustany, Nora. Jordan Expels 21 Iranian Diplomats. Washington Post, February 4,1994. p A26.
[39] Patterns of Global Terrorism: 1993. p.46.

states.[40] Hamas reportedly has an office in Saudi Arabia and, in April 1993, a Hamas delegation visited Qatar to discuss aid to Hamas and the Palestinian people from that Gulf state and the opening of a Hamas political office there.[41] On the other hand, the Saudi and other Persian Gulf governments have been supportive of the Arab-Israeli peace process. Their reluctance to block private contributions to Hamas and Palestinian Islamic Jihad may stem from the unwillingness of the Gulf regimes to offend their wealthy and powerful constituents, or provoke terrorist attacks within their own countries.

Sympathizers in the United States and Europe

A debate over Hamas linkages in the United States began in February 1993 when Israel alleged that Hamas was directing its operations in the occupied territories from U.S.-based command centers. Israel based the charges on information obtained in the January 1993 arrest of two naturalized Arab-Americans (Muhammad Jarad and Muhammad Salah) allegedly for carrying money and instructions from the United States to Hamas activists in the occupied territories. At the time, a State Department spokesman acknowledged that Hamas has sympathizers in the United States but that there was "no evidence to prove that Hamas terrorist operations are working out of the United States."[42] Shortly after these allegations surfaced, some Members of Congress called for investigations of suspected Hamas activity in the United States.[43] The issue flared again following the October 19,1994 bus bombing in Tel Aviv. That day, some Israeli officials reiterated concerns of private U.S. funding for Hamas, although Israel's Ambassador to the United States acknowledged that U.S. law enforcement agencies had worked diligently to curb Hamas activity.[44] On October 24, 1994, Secretary of State Christopher promised a major U.S. effort to cut off private U.S. funding for Hamas, including support for the passage of new legislation, if necessary.[45]

No one is certain how extensive Hamas fundraising activities are in the United States. State Department officials reportedly have said Hamas is receiving "millions" of dollars each year from donors in the United States.[46] Some press

---

[40] Sieff, Martin. U.S. Aims at Hamas' Pocketbook. Washington Times, October 26,1994. p. 1.
[41] Fouad, Ashraf. Hamas Team in Qatar for Political, Financial Aid. Reuters, April 3, 1993.
[42] Nelan, Bruce. Hamas and the Heartland. Time, February 15,1993. pp. 37-8.
[43] See Congressional Record, daily edition, February 2,1993. p. H 320; and February 18,1993. p. S1931.
[44] Itamar Rabinovich Press Conference. Reuters, October 19, 1994.
[45] Worsnip, Patrick. ,U.S. Hints at Laws to Stop Hamas Funding. Reuters, October 24,1994.
[46] Greenhouse, Steven. U.S. Hints at Better Ties if Syria Signs Peace Pact With Israel. New York Times, October 25, 1994. p A8.

reports suggest that Hamas may be receiving one third to forty percent of its budget (estimated by Israeli sources at $30 million per year, see above) from private fundraising in the United States and Britain,[47] but free lance journalist Steven Emerson believes Hamas may get as much as 80 percent of its money from contributors in the United States.[48] Emerson presented his allegations of extensive Hamas fundraising and political activity in the United States on CBS November 13, 1994 edition of "60 Minutes" and in a Public Broadcasting Service special entitled "Jihad in America," on November 21,1994. A former Federal Bureau of Investigation (FBI) official, Oliver Revell, has reported that Islamic organizations in the United States publish and distribute radical Islamic literature in this country and engage in terrorist training operations, and that radical Islamic clerics frequently visit the United States on fundraising drives.[49] The Justice Department position is that fundraising is legal as long as the contributions are not for acts of terrorism. Many Arab-Americans and others contend that the vast majority of the funds raised go toward helping poor Palestinians in the West Bank and Gaza Strip, and are not diverted to any terrorist activity.

IMPLICATIONS FOR U.S. POLICY

For the Clinton Administration, in the wake of the October 1994 Hamas violence against Israel, the immediate question has been how to deny the radical Palestinian Islamic groups outside support. Many contend that, even if outside support were to end, the Palestinian Islamic groups have sufficient support among Palestinians inside the territories to continue operating. Nonetheless, it is widely acknowledged that outside support contributes to their capabilities.

The Administration is likely to have differing degrees of success in blocking outside support for the radical Palestinian Islamic groups. Addressing U.S. efforts to cut off support for Hamas from U.S. sources, a State Department spokeswoman said that a process already is under way "that is aimed at using legal means to cut off domestic material support for terrorist acts committed by Hamas or any other terrorist groups...[The Administration] is reviewing existing U.S. counterterrorism and related laws with a view toward expanding their reach and strengthening enforcement...[The crime bill passed by Congress in August 1994 (H.R. 3355, P.L. 103-322, signed August 25,1994)] contains several provisions that will assist

[47] Sieff, Martin. U.S. Aims at Hamas' Pocketbook. Washington Times, October 26,1994. p.l.
[48] Winer, Todd. Hamas's Chicago Connection. Chicago Jewish News, October 28,1994.
[49] U.S. News and World Report, October 31,1994. p.44; Schweid, Barry. Ex-FBI Official Says U.S. Provides Sanctuary for Muslim Militants; Reuters, November 17,1994.

the counterterrorism effort, including a section (Section 120005) that criminalizes the provision of money and equipment for specific acts of terrorism and [the Administration] will be looking at how that new law might be strengthened."[50] In addition, following the October 19,1994 bus bombing, the State Department Coordinator for Counterterrorism reportedly convened a series of interagency meetings to discuss "all legal means to curb fundraising in the United States for terrorist activities by Hamas and others."[51] Some Members of Congress have supported legislation that would deny Hamas members visas to enter the United States and would stop Hamas fund-raising in the United States. Some analysts have noted that there are substantial legal and political difficulties in trying to curb Hamas fundraising efforts in the United States. Domestic organizations, pursuing any foreign cause, might oppose a measure that could prevent them from raising funds in the United States for peaceful purposes.

As the ultimate guarantor of Persian Gulf security, the United States can exercise substantial leverage on the Gulf states to persuade them to restrict private contributions to Hamas or Palestinian Islamic Jihad. The United States has raised the issue in bilateral U.S.-Saudi discussions,[52] although the short duration of President Clinton's stay in Saudi Arabia and Kuwait during his October 1994 trip to the Middle East precluded his discussing the issue with those leaders, according to a State Department official. In the case of Jordan, the United States could tie foreign aid and debt forgiveness to Jordanian efforts to limit Hamas activity in Jordan and Iranian-Hamas contacts in that country. The United States enjoys somewhat less leverage over Syria, although Syria wants to be removed from the U.S. list of state sponsors of terrorism, which prevents Syria from receiving U.S. foreign aid. U.S. officials have repeatedly said Syria would not be removed from the terrorism list unless and until it ends all support for terrorist groups. Syria's removal will therefore be predicated, at least in part, on its curbing Hamas, Palestinian Islamic Jihad, and Hizballah in Syria or areas of Lebanon under Syrian control. During his October 1994 trip to the Middle East, President Clinton told Syrian President Hafez al-Asad in Damascus that support for terrorist groups is inconsistent with the pursuit of peace with Israel.

The United States has no diplomatic relations with Iran, the Palestinian Islamic groups' most vocal outside supporter. To prevent Iran from building up its strategic arsenal and from spreading its influence abroad, the United States has

---

[50] Sieff, Martin. U.S. Aims at Hamas' Pocketbook. Washington Times, October 26, 1994. p.1

[51] Schweid, Barry. Ex-FBI Official Says U.S. Provides Sanctuary for Muslim Militants. Reuters, November 17,1994.

[52] State Department Briefing. Reuters, June 14, 1994.

relied on a broad package of unilateral sanctions,[53] which includes a ban on aid in any form, controls on U.S. exports of items that could have military applications, and a ban on Iranian imports. Some observers have advocated further U.S. sanctions, including a total ban on U.S. trade with Iran and the prohibition of U.S. oil companies from trading Iranian oil overseas or importing petroleum products made from Iranian oil but refined in countries other than Iran. Some believe the United States should push for U.N. sanctions similar to those imposed on Iraq (for example, a ban on oil exports). Others note little international support for U.N. sanctions on Iran and believe it unlikely that any additional U.S. sanctions would deny Iran the resources to fund radical groups abroad, an activity which is relatively inexpensive.[54]

---

[53] For further information on U.S. efforts to contain Iran, see U.S. Library of Congress. Congressional Research Service. Iran: U.S. Containment Policy. CRS Report 94-652 F, August 11,1994, by Kenneth Katzman. 26 p.

[54] According to one estimate, it costs only about $4,000 per year to fund a two or three man grouping of Palestinian Islamic guerrillas on the West Bank and Gaza Strip. See, Hoffman, David. Hamas' Resilience Surprises Israel. Washington Post, February 3,1993. p. A19.

Chapter 3

THE CURRENT PALESTINIAN UPRISING: AL-AQSA INTIFADAH

Joshua Ruebner, Clyde Mark, Kenneth Katzman and Alfred Prados

INTRODUCTION

Facing a September 13, 2000 deadline for concluding a comprehensive Israeli-Palestinian agreement on all permanent status issues, President Bill Clinton convened a trilateral summit with Israeli Prime Minister Ehud Barak and Palestine Liberation Organization (PLO) Chairman Yasser Arafat at Camp David on July 11, 2000. The summit, which lasted until July 24, 2000, did not produce an agreement.

The relative calm that prevailed in the West Bank and Gaza Strip after the Palestinian Central Council (PCC) decided to delay the declaration of Palestinian statehood on September 10, 2000, evidently masked a deep-seated frustration that many Palestinians felt toward the peace process. This frustration erupted after Likud party head Ariel Sharon led a tour of al-Haram ash-Sharif/Temple Mount on September 28, 2000, which Palestinians and many observers viewed as provocative. The ensuing protests sparked massive clashes involving Palestinian civilians, the Fatah Tanzeem, the Palestinian Authority (PA) police force, Israeli civilians (both Jewish and Arab), and the Israeli police and army. In turn, these clashes have created widespread disillusionment and outrage within the Israeli and Palestinian communities regarding the other's commitment to the peace process.

As of January 10, 2001, 362 people were killed in these clashes, 306 of whom were Palestinians, 43 of whom were Israeli Jews, and 13 of whom were Israeli Arabs.

In addition to this heavy toll of casualties, the Palestinian uprising has also had dramatic economic repercussions. Israel's policy of employing "internal" and "external" closures has wreaked havoc on the fragile Palestinian economy. In turn, Israel has also suffered economically through a loss of tourism revenues and a possible long-term decline in foreign investment. Also, Arab states have donated large sums of money and amounts of humanitarian goods in order to support the intifadah. As a result of the widespread conviction in the Arab world that United States foreign policy is biased toward Israel, a grassroots boycott of U.S. goods has swept the region.

The violence has also spread to Israel's border with Lebanon, triggering fear of a wider conflagration with Lebanon and Syria. Taking advantage of the chaos caused by demonstrations and clashes, Hizballah–a leading Lebanese Shi'ite organization–in a well-planned attack, captured three Israeli soldiers in the disputed Sheba'a Farms region. Hizballah has announced that it wants to exchange the soldiers for Lebanese and other Arab political prisoners currently held in Israeli jails. At this point, it appears that Hizballah is uninterested in opening up a full-fledged second front with Israel. Beyond Lebanon, the uprising has had significant implications, and has drawn widespread Arab and Islamic support for the Palestinian position.

Members of 106th Congress responded to the al-Aqsa Intifadah by introducing bills that supported Israel's actions, encouraged the U.S. Administration to oppose any anti-Israel resolutions in the United Nations, called upon Palestinians to negotiate a resolution, and proposed cutting foreign assistance to the Palestinians if they did not stop the uprising.

Breakdown of the Israeli-Palestinian Peace Process

Facing a deadline that was established in the 1999 Sharm al-Sheikh Memorandum for concluding a comprehensive Israeli-Palestinian agreement on all permanent status issues by September 13, 2000, President Bill Clinton convened a trilateral summit with Israeli Prime Minister Ehud Barak and Palestine Liberation Organization (PLO) Chairman Yasser Arafat at Camp David on July

11, 2000. The summit, which lasted until July 24, 2000, did not produce an agreement.[1]

Although Barak's Camp David proposals included significant new concessions, Arafat rejected the offers. In Arafat's view, these proposals fell short of meeting minimum Palestinian requirements and aspirations for a comprehensive agreement, embodied in U.N. General Assembly Resolution 194, which recognizes the Palestinian refugees' right of return, and Security Council Resolution 242, which calls upon Israel to withdraw from territories occupied during the 1967 Arab-Israeli War. Nonetheless, the summit narrowed the wide gaps that had existed on several permanent status issues. According to various press accounts, Barak offered Arafat (1) some form of custodianship over al-Haram ash-Sharif/Temple Mount (see below) and administrative autonomy for Palestinian neighborhoods in East Jerusalem, (2) the return of between 80,000-100,000 refugees in the context of 'family reunification' without recognizing the 'right of return,' (3) the dismantling of some Israeli settlements in the West Bank and Gaza Strip or their reversion to Palestinian sovereignty, and (4) a withdrawal from 100% of the Gaza Strip and between 88-94% of the West Bank. On his part, Arafat reportedly agreed to (1) recognize Israeli sovereignty over parts of East Jerusalem, including the Jewish Quarter of the Old City, (2) recognize the impracticality of implementing the Palestinian refugees' right of return, (3) allow Israel to annex three blocs of settlements in the West Bank in exchange for territory within Israel proper, and (4) settle for less than a return of all Palestinian territory conquered by Israel in 1967.[2]

Although low-level negotiations continued after the Camp David summit, the two sides were unable to reach an agreement before the September 13 deadline. On September 10, under pressure from foreign countries and realizing that a unilateral declaration of statehood would likely precipitate harsh Israeli counter-measures, the Palestinian Central Council (PCC) decided to delay a declaration of Palestinian statehood, continue negotiations with Israel, and revisit the statehood issue by mid- November (which coincided with the November 15th anniversary of the Palestinian National Council's symbolic declaration of independence in 1988).[3] This was the second time that the PCC delayed declaring the independence of the Palestinian state: it also delayed making this declaration after

[1] For further details, see CRS Report RS20648, *Israeli-Palestinian Peace Process: Camp David Negotiations*, by Jeannie Sowers, August 3, 2000.

[2] For the most comprehensive first-hand account of the Camp David summit to date, see Akram Hanieh, "The Camp David Papers," *al-Ayyam*, August 2000. These papers were a seven-part serial published in the Palestinian daily newspaper *al-Ayyam* between July 27-August 10, 2000.

[3] The complete text of the PCC's statement is reprinted in "The Text of the Closing Statement of the Meeting of the Palestinian Central Council," *al-Hayat*, September 12, 2000.

the interim period of the Israeli- Palestinian peace process expired on May 4, 1999.

The relative calm that prevailed in the West Bank and Gaza Strip following the delay of Palestinian statehood evidently masked a deep-seated frustration that many Palestinians felt toward the peace process. After seven years of interim negotiations and agreements whose provisions often went unimplemented, and frequently missed deadlines for concluding a permanent status agreement, many Palestinians apparently came to believe that the peace process would never reach a conclusion that met their minimum aspirations and requirements as embodied in relevant U.N. Security Council resolutions. This disillusionment with the peace process deepened after Barak revealed his outline for a permanent status agreement at Camp David; an outline that did not meet popular Palestinian goals of achieving complete sovereignty over East Jerusalem, fully implementing the Palestinian refugees' right of return, and regaining all Palestinian territories conquered by Israel in 1967. This latent discontent over the course and future of the peace process set the stage for potential Israeli-Palestinian clashes. The proximate cause that triggered these clashes occurred on September 28, 2000.

Within Israel, the two camps, those supporting Camp David and those opposed, appeared to become more polarized. A public opinion poll, conducted shortly after Camp David ended, showed that 66% of Israelis continued to support the peace process, and 29% opposed further talks with the Palestinians. But the right wing grew more adamant in its opposition to the Camp David talks and to Israel relinquishing control over Jerusalem and more of the occupied territories, or agreeing to the Palestinian refugees' right of return. General Israeli dissatisfaction with Barak and his coalition appeared to be growing.

ASPECTS OF THE ISRAELI-PALESTINIAN VIOLENCE

Confrontation in Jerusalem

On September 28, 2000, Likud Party leader and former defense minister Ariel Sharon led a Likud party Knesset contingent, guarded by 1,000 riot-gear clad Israeli police, on a tour of al-Haram ash-Sharif/Har HaBayt (Noble Sanctuary/Temple Mount) religious area in the Old City of Jerusalem. Jews revere the Temple Mount as the site of the First and Second Temples. Muslims revere the Noble Sanctuary as the terminus for Muhammad's visit to heaven and as the current site of the al-Aqsa Mosque and the Dome of the Rock. Muslims have controlled al-Haram ash-Sharif/Har HaBayt since defeating the Crusaders in the 12th century. Since Israel occupied the area in 1967, Israeli authorities have made the site off limits to groups of Jews who attempt to demonstrate or pray there because of the possibility of upsetting Muslim sensibilities. Also, in obedience to many rabbinical decisions, some Jews will not enter the area because they fear that they might inadvertently walk on sacred ground. Jews, however, do pray at the adjacent Western (or Wailing) Wall, which, as an outer retaining wall of the structure that supported the Second Temple, is considered to be sacred.

Sharon described his visit as an exercise of his rights as a Jew and an Israeli to visit sites sacred to Judaism,[4] a stance supported by many Israelis. Others speculated that Sharon intended his visit to derail the peace process by antagonizing the Palestinians, thereby creating confrontations that would compel Israel to withdraw the concessions offered at Camp David. Palestinians particularly dislike Sharon because of his role in the Israel Defense Forces' (IDF) Unit 101, which often attacked Arab villages in the 1950s, and his role as Defense Minister during Israel's invasion of Lebanon in 1982, when he was indirectly implicated in the massacre of Palestinian civilians at the Sabra and Shatilla refugee camps, near Beirut. Some suspected that Sharon's visit was an attempt to weaken further the Barak government, or to strengthen Sharon's position in an anticipated contest with former Prime Minister Binyamin Netanyahu for leadership of the Likud party.

After Sharon's tour of the Noble Sanctuary/Temple Mount, 200 to 300 Palestinians began throwing stones at the accompanying police. By the next day, September 29, 2000, the confrontation spread to other areas of the occupied territories, including the West Bank towns of Qalqilya, Bethlehem, Hebron, and Ramallah, and the Netzarim junction in the Gaza Strip, and on October 1, fighting broke out between Israeli Jews and Israeli Arabs in Nazareth, Umm al-Fahm, and Jaffa inside Israel. Israeli police used tear gas, rubber-coated bullets, and live ammunition against the demonstrators' stones, fire bombs, and rifle and pistol fire. On October 1, Israeli helicopter gun ships fired on Palestinian sniper locations in apartment buildings near the Netzarim junction after Palestinian snipers started shooting at the Israeli military post. The same day, Israeli tanks moved to the outskirts of Nablus and to the area near Joseph's Tomb to protect the Israeli military post and religious seminary in the area.[5] Tanks and helicopters

[4] "Q&A: Ariel Sharon; My Visit Didn't Cause the Violence," *Washington Post*, October 8, 2000.

[5] The Israelis abandoned the site on October 7, and Arab rioters burned the Jewish religious seminary there. Keith Richburg, "Palestinians Proclaim a Victory," *Washington Post*, October 8, 2000, and "Who Is Buried in Embattled Shrine: Joseph or Muslim Sheik?," *Associated Press*, October 11, 2000.

appeared outside Bethlehem, Hebron, Ramallah, and other West Bank cities. There were reports of incidents in which the Palestinian police joined forces with the Arab rioters and attacked Israelis, and of Israeli police joining Israeli Jews attacking Arabs in Israel.[6]

Excessive Force Issue

By January 5, 2001, Palestinians had killed 21 Israeli military and 22 Israeli civilians. Israeli police killed 13 Israeli Arabs in the incidents inside Israel. In the same period, September 28 through January 5, Israeli military and settlers killed 300 Palestinian Arabs. More than 400 Israelis and 12,000 Palestinians have been injured in the fighting.

The lopsided nature of the casualty figures and Israel's use of live ammunition, tanks, and helicopters prompted Israeli, Palestinian, and international human rights organizations to accuse Israel of employing disproportionate levels of force in trying to restore order.[7] On November 21, 2000, State Department spokesman Richard Boucher said "... we expect (the Palestinian Authority) to do all they can to stop the violence and restore calm. In addition, while we are pressing the Palestinians, we think the Israelis also need to understand that the use of excessive force is not the right way to go."[8] Israeli authorities argued that strong measures were needed to contain the violence, and some Israelis criticized the government for not responding with even greater force. Israeli military commanders repeatedly issued orders to shoot to kill when Israeli lives were in danger. The Israeli shoot to kill rules of engagement applied equally to armed Palestinians and to rock throwers.

The Palestinians claim that between September 28, 2000, and January 4, 2001, Israeli armed forces or intelligence officers assassinated 20 Palestinian activists using drive-by shootings, long-range sniper fire, car bombs, tank fire, or helicopter gunships.[9] Most of the activists were members of Fatah, Yasser Arafat's mainstream wing of the PLO, while a few were Islamists who belonged to either Hamas or Islamic Jihad and who had been imprisoned by the Palestinian

---

[6] Marjorie Miller, "Hatreds Erupt as Scores of Youths Rampage Through an Arab Neighborhood in Retaliation," *Los Angeles Times*, October 10, 2000.

[7] Various organizations have issued reports: for example the Israeli organization B'Tselem on October 6, Human Rights Watch on October 17, and Amnesty International in October and November.

[8] Department of State daily press briefing. November 21, 2000.

[9] "Palestinian Activist Slain, the Third in 3 Days," *Boston Globe*, December 14, 2000, and "Israeli Troops Kill Palestinian Militants," *Reuters*, December 21, 2000.

Authority (PA) but released during the first week of the intifadah. On December 17, a senior Israeli Defense Force (IDF) officer confirmed that Israel had adopted a policy of tracking down some Palestinian intifadah activists and killing them.[10]

"Icons" of the Battle

On September 30, 2000, 12-year-old Muhammad Jamal al-Durrah of Briej refugee camp was killed by Israeli forces firing from a police post at Palestinian demonstrators. Pictures of the frightened boy and his father crouched behind a barrel to avoid the shooting and then succumbing to the gunfire became a Palestinian icon symbolizing innocent Palestinians at the mercy of Israeli force. On October 12, two Israeli soldiers were arrested by Palestinian police in Ramallah and taken to the Ramallah police headquarters. A mob stormed the police station, stabbed to death the two Israelis, and threw one of the bodies out a second story window. Israeli television relayed the vivid pictures of Palestinians beating the two dead Israelis and a Palestinian youth proudly holding aloft his bloody hands. Pictures of the bloody hands and the mutilated Israeli became Israel's icon of Palestinian brutality.

Israelis said Muhammad al-Durrah was caught in a cross-fire, implying that either Palestinian or Israeli bullets may have killed the boy. Palestinians maintained that there were no Palestinians firing in the area and that the boy was killed by Israeli gunfire. Israel said the two Israelis killed in Ramallah were army reservists who lost their way and wandered into an area under Palestinian police control, and that Palestinian police authorities did nothing to stop the murderous mob. Palestinians alleged that the two men were members of an Israeli military unit that regularly dress in civilian clothes to kidnap or kill Palestinian activists. Also a local Palestinian police commander maintained that he tried unsuccessfully to protect the two Israelis. Israel responded to the Ramallah incident with helicopter rocket attacks against the police headquarters and Palestinian Authority offices in Ramallah, and a police station and coast guard headquarters in Gaza, and tightened the closure in the occupied territories.

---

[10] Richburg, Keith B., Israelis Confirm Assassinations Used as Policy, Washington Post, January 8, 2001, A1, A12. "IDF Officer Confirms Targeting 'Terrorists'; Suspected Collaborators Slain in PA," *Voice of Israel*, December 21, 2000. *Voice of Israel* is a government-owned radio station.

Diplomacy

On October 2, 2000, U.S. Secretary of State Madeleine Albright announced that Arafat and Barak would meet with her in Paris to seek a cease-fire. At the October 4 meetings, which also included French President Jacques Chirac and U.N. Secretary General Kofi Annan, Arafat and Barak ordered their military and police commanders to pull back from confrontational points and appealed for an end to the violence, but the two could not agree on a mechanism for investigating the causes of the conflict. Arafat wanted an international effort, perhaps led by a U.N. team, to investigate and report on Israeli actions in the conflict, and Barak wanted a U.S.-led investigation into the causes of the conflict. Israel withdrew its tanks from points near Nablus, Bethlehem, Ramallah, and other sites, but the deadly exchanges continued.

Following the Paris meetings, Arafat and Secretary Albright went to Sharm al-Shaykh to meet with Egyptian President Hosni Mubarak in the hope that he could advance the cause of peace, but the meeting ended without result when Barak refused to attend. Meanwhile, the United States had been negotiating at the United Nations to frame a resolution that would call for an end to the fighting without casting blame. On October 7, the United States abstained on U.N. Security Council Resolution 1322, which deplored the provocation that led to the fighting, and called for an end to the conflict and a resumption of the peace negotiations. Annan, United Kingdom Foreign Secretary Robin Cook, Russian Foreign Minister Igor Ivanov, and European Union official Javier Solana joined the French and U.S. Presidents in seeking an end to the fighting and a resumption of the peace talks.

Intensive diplomatic negotiations led to the convening of a summit at the Egyptian resort town of Sharm al-Shaykh on October 16-17, 2000. The summit, hosted by Mubarak, chaired by President Clinton, and attended by Barak, Arafat, Annan, Solana, and King Abdullah of Jordan, aimed at achieving a cease fire and agreeing upon a format for an international investigation of the incidents. After 24 hours of meetings, President Clinton read a three-part statement summarizing an agreement: first, that Barak and Arafat would issue statements calling for an end to the violence; second, that a U.S.-led fact finding mission in consultation with the United Nations would report on the events of the past several weeks; and third, that the United States would consult with Israel and the Palestinians on resuming the peace negotiations. Under the first point, President Clinton listed actions that would end the confrontation, such as restoring law and order, enhancing security cooperation (both apparently aimed at the Palestinians), pulling back armed forces from points of friction, ending the closure of

Palestinian areas, and re-opening Gaza airport (apparently aimed at Israel). The formula for the fact-finding mission appeared to compromise between Israel's preference for a U.S.-led fact-finding group and the Palestinian preference for a U.N. investigation of the three-week confrontation.

On November 8, 2000, President Clinton named five men to serve on the fact-finding commission mentioned at Paris and Sharm al-Shaykh: former U.S. Senators George Mitchell and Warren Rudman, former Turkish President Suleman Demirel, Norwegian Foreign Minister Thorgboern Jagland, and European Union Chief of Security and Policy Javier Solana. The commission was to review the current crisis with the objective of preventing a recurrence. The commission began its investigation on December 10, with the intention of submitting its report in March 2001. Critics suggested that the commission began too late, was operating with a vague purpose, and would produce a useless document.

President Clinton met at the White House with Chairman Arafat on November 9 and with Prime Minister Barak on November 12, but the meetings produced no peace process breakthroughs and no cease-fire in the uprising. Reports in the Palestinian and Israeli press said the two sides continued meeting in private, away from public scrutiny. Meanwhile, the Palestinians advocated placing an international force of observers in the occupied territories to report on Israeli actions and to protect the Palestinians. Israel opposed an international presence unless there was an agreement to end the violence. A resolution to create the proposed international observer force failed to receive the necessary nine votes in the U.N. Security Council on December 18. At the invitation of President Clinton, Palestinian and Israeli negotiators met at Bolling Air Force base outside Washington on December 19, but with the difference that almost immediately, rumors began circulating that they were making progress.

A December change in the peace dynamic may be attributed, in part, to the changing Israeli political scene. Prime Minister Barak announced on December 9 that he would resign the next day. Under Israeli law, his resignation became official on December 12, to be followed by an election for prime minister in 60 days. Barak's opponent in the February 6, 2001 election is Ariel Sharon, head of the Likud Party, considered by most analysts to be a hawk opposed to the Oslo peace process and to surrendering any West Bank or Gaza land to a Palestinian state. Observers speculated that Barak wanted to complete the peace process, hoping to run as the prime minister who delivered a peace agreement. Also, others speculated that Arafat would be amenable to a peace agreement under Barak, fearing that a Sharon government would rescind pending Israeli offers and reverse the Oslo process.[11]

Arafat met with President Clinton at the White House on January 2, 2001, to discuss a cease-fire and the President's proposal for peace. Arafat replied on January 4 from Cairo that the PLO accepted the Clinton proposal "with reservations." Israel had accepted the Clinton proposal, also with "reservations", the week before. Theoretically, it is possible to arrange a cease-fire and a peace agreement before Clinton leaves office on January 20, but pragmatically, it appears unlikely.

ECONOMIC CONSEQUENCES OF THE PALESTINIAN UPRISING

The following section highlights some of the more pertinent economic consequences of the intifidah. It does not purport to offer any total estimates of the economic costs to date.

Palestinian Economy

Israel has responded to the Palestinian uprising by frequently employing "internal closures" and "external closures" of the occupied Palestinian territories. Under an "internal closure," the Israeli military surrounds and "seals" individual Palestinian villages, refugee camps, and cities thereby preventing the flow of goods and people between Palestinian areas and inhibiting normal commercial and financial transactions and labor mobility. Under an "external closure," the Israeli military "seals" the West Bank and Gaza Strip from each other, from Israel, and from the outside world. The "external closure" prevents any economic interaction between the West Bank and Gaza Strip, precludes the approximately 120,000 Palestinians employed in Israel before the outbreak of the Palestinian uprising from reaching their jobs across the Green Line, and stops Palestinian trade with the rest of the world because the Palestinians do not have an independent import-export route outside of Israel's control. Israel maintains that its closure policy is designed to reduce general security risks by limiting Palestinians from entering Israel.[12] Critics, however, say that Palestinians who

[11] For further details on the Israeli election campaign, see CRS Report RS20753, *Israel: 2001 Elections*, by Clyde Mark and Joshua Ruebner, updated January 3, 2001.

[12] According to the Israeli Foreign Ministry, "the purpose of the closure policy is not punitive, but has become necessary to ensure the security of Israeli citizens in these trying times." Quoted from "The Current Situation in Israel–Answers to Frequently Asked Questions," November 9, 2000,

benefit from access to the Israeli labor market have rarely engaged in acts detrimental to Israel's security, and Palestinians who have harmed Israel's security generally have been able to evade Israeli closures, especially through the West Bank, which is difficult, if not impossible, to "hermetically seal" from Israel. Palestinians claim that Israel's closure policy is not designed to address its security concerns; rather, they claim that the policy is a form of "collective punishment" that is designed to purposefully inflict damage on the Palestinian economy in order to put pressure on the Palestinians to adhere to Israel's political agenda.

As on previous occasions when Israel has employed its closure policy, the results have been devastating for the Palestinian economy. In mid-December 2000, the UN released a report that documented global losses to the Palestinian economy during the first two months of the intifadah totaling more than $500 million.[13] The UN noted that this total represented an estimated loss of 10% of Palestinian gross domestic product (GDP) projected for 2000 and was more than 250% of the value of donor disbursements to the Palestinian Authority (PA) in the first half of 2000. PA President Yasser Arafat has estimated even larger losses to the Palestinian economy stemming from the intifadah: at an emergency meeting of Arab Labor Ministers on November 23, 2000, Arafat declared that the intifadah had cost the Palestinian economy $800 million.[14]

Rising unemployment, resulting in higher levels of poverty, has been perhaps the most prominent feature of the intifadah's impact upon the Palestinian economy. As noted above, Israel's "external closure" of the West Bank and Gaza Strip has prevented Palestinian workers from reaching their former jobs inside the Green Line. The Governor of the Palestinian Monetary Authority, Dr. Fouad Beseiso, has estimated that this costs the Palestinian labor force $4.5 million daily in lost wages and has led to unemployment levels of up to 50%.[15] Even when Israel slightly relaxed its external closure policy in mid-December by re-issuing 6,000 work permits for the Gaza Strip and 9,000 permits for the West Bank, only

---

retrieved from Israel's Ministry of Foreign Affairs website, at [http://www.israel.org/mfa/go.asp?MFAH0i9o0].

[13] "The Impact on the Palestinian Economy of Confrontations, Mobility Restrictions and Border Closures, 28 September-26 November 2000," Office of the United Nations Special Co-Ordinator, retrieved from the Palestinian National Authority Official Website at [http://www/pna.net/un/un_pal_economy.htm]. Unless otherwise indicated, all statistics in this section come from this report.

[14] Jabir al-Qarmooti, "Arafat at the Emergency Conference of Arab Labor Ministers: $800 Million Losses to Our Economy since September," *al-Hayat*, November 23, 2000.

[15] "The Palestinian Economy in the Shadow of the Intifadah: Losses Exceeding What the Donor Countries Have Provided by Several Times," *al-Hayat*, November 9, 2000.

a few thousand Palestinians took up the offer and returned to work within Israel.[16] The apparent dearth of Palestinian workers who want to return to their jobs in Israel at present could imply one of two things: either Palestinians fear for their personal security in Israel in the present climate or they are re-evaluating their economic dependence on the Israeli labor market and the costs that this entails. "Internal closures" have also negatively affected the Palestinian labor force. According to one estimate, 97% of Palestinian companies have experienced slowdowns because many employees have not been able to reach their places of employment due to internal closures.[17]

Although all sectors of the Palestinian economy have been damaged by the intifadah and the resultant closures, the agricultural and tourism sectors have been hard hit. Both sectors are particularly vulnerable to exogenous shocks: the agricultural sector is subject to time sensitivities regarding the harvesting and marketing of produce and the tourism sector is subject to the security concerns and perceptions of tourists and travel agents. As a result of closures, Palestinians were largely unable to harvest their fields and much of the fall crop rotted in the field. Furthermore, Palestinians found it very difficult to market the portion of the harvest that was salvageable because, as mentioned above, external closures prevented Palestinian exports from reaching their intended destinations. Mohammed Shtayyeh, Director of the Palestinian Economic Council for Development and Reconstruction (PECDAR), estimated that the agricultural sector suffered losses of $120 million.[18] Anecdotal evidence suggests that the tourism sector is facing an even more serious collapse. For instance, in Bethlehem, where the PA recently invested $200 million to expand the city's tourism infrastructure, most hotels have been closed for a lack of guests and many services associated with tourism–restaurants, souvenir shops, etc.–have reported a sharp loss of business.[19]

The first intifadah (1987-1993) led many Palestinians to rebel against what they viewed as an unjust relationship of economic dependence on Israel. This rebellion was characterized by a widespread refusal to remit taxes to an occupying

---

[16] Amos Harel, "Only a Few Thousand Workers Entered Israel from the [Occupied] Territories," *Ha'aretz*, December 18, 2000.

[17] Na'im Nasser, "97% of Palestinian Companies Suffer from an Absence of Their Employees," *al-Hayat*, November 20, 2000.

[18] Mary Curtius, "Olive Harvest Becomes a Palestinian Casualty," *Los Angeles Times*, November 25, 2000.

[19] Stephen J. Glain, "Bethlehem Struggles with Too Much Room at the Inns–Tourists, Key to the Economy, Stay Away This Year Amid Israeli-Palestinian Conflict," *Wall Street Journal*, December 20, 2000.

authority that rarely reinvested this money for the benefit of the Palestinian people and by popular boycotts of Israeli consumer goods that often were perceived to flood a captive market, undercut nascent Palestinian industry, and contribute to the perpetuation of the occupation. Similarly, the current intifadah appears to have caused many Palestinians to reevaluate their continued economic dependence on Israel as a source of employment and as its largest trading partner. As noted above, the fact that only a few Palestinian workers who have been re-issued work permits to work in Israel have returned to their jobs could point to an emerging trend regarding the desirability of this type of employment. Also, both on an official and popular level, there have been attempts to reduce imports of Israeli goods and diversify Palestinian trade patterns.[20] This reevaluation could cast doubts upon the feasibility of plans for close economic relations between Israel and the future State of Palestine under a permanent status peace treaty.

Israeli Economy

The Palestinian uprising has also contributed to a worsening of economic conditions in Israel. Though gross losses to the Israeli economy could exceed gross losses to the Palestinian economy, the relative sizes of the two economies–Israel's GDP ($99 billion) was roughly 25 times greater than Palestinian GDP ($4 billion) in 1999–have meant that the per capita impact has been much greater on the Palestinian economy. By some estimates, the Israeli economy lost more than $1 billion within a month of the outbreak of the intifadah.[21] Overall Israeli losses from the intifadah are expected to reach as high as $2.25 billion, and the Governor of the Bank of Israel, Dr. David Klein, has downgraded GDP growth projections for 2001by 1-2% as a result.[22]

The external closure imposed by Israel on the West Bank and Gaza Strip has disturbed the sectors of the Israeli economy that rely upon Palestinian labor, especially the agricultural and construction sectors. The external closure has resulted in an immediate supply-side labor shortage, causing wages in these sectors to rise dramatically. According to one report, the resultant high demand for foreign (non-Palestinian) workers in these sectors has caused wages to roughly

---

[20] See, for instance, Wafa Amr, "Palestinians to Boycott Israeli Goods," *Reuters*, October 7, 2000, and Ora Coren, "PA to Shift to Imports from Arab States and Europe," *Ha'aretz*, October 25, 2000.

[21] As'ad Telhami, "Losses to Israel since the Intifadah Surpass $1 Billion," *al-Hayat*, October 26, 2000.

[22] Yossi Greenstein, "Klein: The Security Events Will Cause a Loss of Up to 9 Billion Shekels in GDP in 2001," *Ma'ariv*, December 8, 2000.

double.[23] If accurate, such wage hikes could place inflationary pressures on the economy as a whole in the longer term.

Particularly hard hit by the effects of the Palestinian uprising has been the tourism sector in Israel. Year-on-year statistics released by Israel's Central Bureau of Statistics show that the number of tourists arriving in Israel dropped by 33% in October and by 46% in November compared to 1999. Also, El Al, Israel's national airline, has reported operating losses of $20 million in these two months and 15,000 hotel employees have been laid off.[24]

Foreign investors may attach a high risk premium to countries experiencing political violence; therefore, the Palestinian uprising could also have the long-term effect of making Israel a less attractive place for foreign direct investment (FDI) and might make it more difficult for Israeli companies to attract portfolio investments. Although the impact of the intifadah on the business plans of foreign companies investing in Israel is unclear, there are early indications that the intifadah is taking a toll on Israeli companies listed on foreign stock markets. For instance, according to one report, Israeli technology stocks listed on NASDAQ lost $20 billion in value during the first two months of the intifidah.[25]

The outbreak of the intifadah has spurred calls, on both the Israeli and Palestinian sides, for a geographic and economic "separation" of the two nations. As a spinoff to this call for separating the two economies, at the popular level, some Israeli Jews have called for "breaking off economic relations" with Israel's Palestinian Arab citizens in retaliation for their show of solidarity with their Palestinian brethren in the occupied territories. For instance, in Tel Aviv, flyers were distributed calling upon Jews to boycott Arab-owned restaurants, and the Israeli rabbinate revoked the *kashrut* licenses[26] of 16 Arab-owned food processing factories, thus effectively shutting them out of the Israeli Jewish market and placing them in danger of bankruptcy.[27] An extended and wide spread boycott of the Israeli Arab sectors of the economy by Israeli Jews could cast long-term doubts about the future of coexistence between the two communities in Israel.

---

[23] "The Israeli Manufacturing Sector is Suffering from the Effects of Preventing Palestinian Workers from Reaching Their Places of Work," *al-Quds al-'Arabi*, December 5, 2000.

[24] David Rosenberg, "Palestinian Unrest Takes Growing Toll on Israeli Tourism," *Dow Jones*, December 27, 2000.

[25] Mohammad Khalid, "$20 Billion Losses for Israeli Technology Companies in American Financial Markets since the Beginning of 'the al-Aqsa Intifadah'," *al-Hayat*, November 24, 2000. If the drop is related only to the unrest, or is part of a general downturn in the NASDAQ is arguable.

[26] These licences attest that the food is kosher and that its preparation adheres to the principles of Jewish dietary law, *kashrut*.

[27] Sa'id Badran and Iti Asher, "An Account of the Riots: A Jewish Consumers' Boycott Results in Arab-Owned Stores and Restaurants Remaining Empty," *Ma'ariv*, October 25, 2000.

Arab Assistance

The outbreak of the al-Aqsa Intifadah has triggered a wave of pan-Arab solidarity with the Palestinian people (see below for further details). To date, the Arab world, both at the popular and government levels, has pledged large sums of money and donated large quantities of humanitarian goods to the Palestinians both to give expression to this solidarity and to try to counteract the adverse economic consequences of the uprising.

The largest such initiative to date stemmed from resolutions approved at the Arab League summit, held in Cairo on October 22, 2000. At this summit, which was convened for the express purpose of addressing the intifadah and Israel's response to it, the Arab states agreed to establish two funds, totaling $1 billion, to support the Palestinian uprising. The larger of the two funds, the al-Quds (Jerusalem) Fund, is to total $800 million, and is to be used to protect the Arab and Islamic character of East Jerusalem. The smaller of the funds, the al-Aqsa Intifadah Fund, is to total $200 million, and is intended to support directly Palestinian families that have suffered casualties in the uprising.

As of late November, subscriptions to the two funds were nearly three-quarters filled. Table 1, below, details the contributions that various Arab countries have pledged to the funds so far. Of these total pledges, it is difficult to determine how much money has actually flowed into these funds to date. Also, several governmental and popular initiatives have resulted in pledges and donations to the Palestinians outside the framework of these two funds.

Monies pledged to these funds are not direct cash transfers to the Palestinian Authority (PA) or the Palestine Liberation Organization (PLO). Rather, at a follow-up meeting of Arab Finance Ministers, it was decided that all contributions to these funds would flow through and be administered by the respected Saudi Arabian-based Islamic Development Bank (IDB).[28] Though the Palestinian leadership might have hoped to directly receive money from these funds, some Arab states may have harbored worries that this money could have been misappropriated if handed to the PA, an institution often accused of corruption. Also, some of the Gulf states may have been reluctant to directly fund the PLO or PLO-led institutions because of Yasser Arafat's backing of Iraq during the Gulf War. For instance, Kuwait's Foreign Minister, Sheikh Sabah al-Ahmad, had to allay the concerns of some Kuwaiti parliamentarians that funding the PA would "damage our [Kuwaiti] sovereignty and security" by promising that none of

---

[28] "The Administration of the al-Aqsa and al-Quds Funds Rests Upon the Islamic Development Bank," *al-Hayat*, November 25, 2000.

Kuwait's contributions would flow directly to the PA.[29] The designation of the IDB as the administrator of these funds neatly sidestepped these issues by allowing Arab states to financially support the intifadah (and respond to domestic constituencies that often aggressively challenged their governments to confront Israel's attempt to suppress the uprising) while avoiding the political difficulties entailed in directly funding the PA. On December 21, the IDB approved an initial five projects totaling $7.5 million.[30]

Table 1. Pledges to the Al-Quds and Al-Aqsa Intifadah Funds

Country	Amount
Saudi Arabia	$250 million
Kuwait	$150 million
United Arab Emirates	$150 million
Qatar	$50 million
Algeria	$30 million
Egypt	$30 million
Yemen	$10 million
Oman	$10 million
Syria	$7 million
Bahrain	$3 million
Jordan	$2 million
Sudan	$1 million
Total	**$693 million**

Source: *al-Hayat*, November 25, 2000.

Arab Boycott of U.S. Goods

In addition to spurring a wave of pan-Arab solidarity with the Palestinian cause, the al-Aqsa Intifadah has also occasioned a popular backlash against United States foreign policy in the Middle East, which most, if not all, Arabs consider to be biased toward Israel and built on double standards regarding the enforcement of international law. One of the most visible and prominent aspects of this backlash against U.S. support for Israel has come in the form of a boycott of U.S. goods. Newly-formed popular committees, non-governmental

---

[29] Hamad al-Jassir, "Sabah al-Ahmad: Mechanism for the Money of the al-Aqsa and Intifadah Funds [*sic*] and the [Palestinian] Authority Will Not Receive It," *al-Hayat*, November 7, 2000.

[30] "Islamic Bank Says $7.5 Million Approved for Palestinians," *Reuters*, December 21, 2000.

organizations (NGOs), and professional unions throughout the Arab world have published "black lists" of goods to boycott and guides on how to find local alternatives to popular American products.[31] Although to date the boycott movement has remained decentralized and coordinated differently within each Arab country, it is possible that in the future a more coordinated pan-Arab boycott movement could arise.[32]

Several prominent Muslim clerics issued *fatawa* (singular *fatwa*, or Islamic religious ruling) that lent the boycott campaign a degree of religious legitimation. The *fatawa* forbid the purchase of American products on the grounds that American money supports Israel's military and that therefore the United States is indirectly responsible for Israel's killing of Palestinians. Some of the more significant *fatawa* have been issued by Sheikh Yussef al-Qardawi, an Egyptian-born scholar living in Qatar who has a widespread following throughout the Arab and Islamic world; Dr. Mohammad Sayyid Tantawi, Sheikh of al-Azhar University, which is located in Cairo and is the oldest and one of the most well-respected religious institutions in the Islamic world; and Sheikh Fareed Wassel Nasser, the Grand Mufti of Egypt.

Although it is unclear if this boycott will have long term effects on U.S. exports to the region, there are reports that this movement has produced a dramatic decline in demand for brand-name, easily-identifiable American products and franchises, including fast-food restaurants, bottled beverages, cigarettes, cleaning products, and shoes. For instance, in Egypt, profits at American fast-food restaurants have reportedly dropped 35%, while in Saudi Arabia, business at American fast-food restaurants has reportedly decreased by 64%.[33]

Although the Western media has tended to disparage the importance of the boycott,[34] it is fairly clear that those participating in the boycott do so out of ideological conviction and perceive it to be an effective way to attempt to influence U.S. policy on a popular level. Over and above any economic impact, the boycott movement points to a widespread and growing political disconnect

---

[31] For instance, see, Mohammad Salah, "An Egyptian Black List...for American Goods," *al-Hayat*, October 17, 2000, and "Jordanian Manual Guides the Citizen on How to Boycott American Products and Where to Obtain Alternatives," *al-Quds al-'Arabi*, December 11, 2000.

[32] "The Arab People Revive the Boycott Weapon," *al-Osbou'a al-'Arabi*, December 25, 2000.

[33] "Egypt: Official *Fatwa* Boycotting Products of America and Israel and a Discovery of Two Mossad Spies Raises Tensions with Tel Aviv," *al-Quds al-'Arabi*, November 29, 2000, and 'Amr az-Zubeidi, "Secretary General of Saudi Chambers [of Commerce] Calls for a Transformation of the Positive Boycott of American Goods into a Demand for Goods of Companies Supporting Arab Rights," *ash-Sharq al-Awsat*, December 28, 2000.

[34] For instance, see, Rawhi Abeidoh, "Arab Push to Boycott U.S. Products Only Symbolic," *Reuters*, November 28, 2000.

between the objectives of the Arab world and its perception of U.S. foreign policy biases.

SPREAD OF VIOLENCE TO LEBANON

In solidarity with Palestinians in the West Bank and Gaza Strip, Palestinian refugees in Lebanon held protests against Israel's policies on the Israeli-Lebanese border on October 7. (Since Israel withdrew from its self-declared 'security zone' in south Lebanon in May 2000, the Israeli-Lebanese border has remained tense. Lebanese and Palestinians have thrown rocks and other objects at Israeli soldiers on the other side of the border and the soldiers have occasionally opened fire to quell the protests.) During this protest, Palestinian rock throwing prompted Israeli soldiers to open fire on the demonstrators, killing two of them.[35]

Taking advantage of the ensuing mayhem, Hizballah initiated a well-planned operation to capture Israeli soldiers. Under the cover of smoke bombs and more than 300 rounds of mortar and rocket fire that it directed against Israeli positions, several Hizballah fighters stormed a border gate in the contested Sheba'a Farms region and captured three Israeli soldiers who were on a routine patrol.[36] Israel responded with cross-border aerial attacks. On October 15, Hizballah secretary general Sayyid Hassan Nasrallah announced that his organization now held in custody a fourth Israeli. According to various versions of the incident, the person in question is either a businessman, an arms-dealer, a colonel in the Israeli reserves, or a Mossad agent. He apparently was either kidnapped in Switzerland in early October and eventually transferred to Hizballah, or was lured to Lebanon by Hizballah agents and abducted there. Details of the incident remain sketchy.

Hizballah has announced that it wants to exchange the kidnapped Israeli soldiers for Lebanese and other Arab political prisoners who are being held in Israeli jails. Currently, Israel is holding 19 Lebanese prisoners, the most prominent of whom are Mustafa al-Dirani and Sheikh 'Abd al-Karim 'Obeid, of Hizballah and Amal respectively, who were kidnapped from their homes in Lebanon in order to extract information about Israeli MIA Ron Arad. Also, the Palestinian Authority (PA) reportedly sent Hizballah a list of over 1,100 Palestinian political prisoners held in Israeli jails, in the hope that these prisoners will be included in an eventual swap. Furthermore, Hizballah has received a list of

---

[35] "Israeli Army Kills Palestinians at Lebanon Border," *Reuters*, October 7, 2000.

[36] For a description of the operation, see John Kifner, "A Plan, a Smoke Cloud and 3 Were Gone," *New York Times*, October 12, 2000.

32 Israeli Arabs who are being held in Israeli jails as 'security prisoners'.[37] Hizballah appears to want to exchange the four Israelis for all Arab prisoners held in Israeli jails. Toward this end, Hizballah secretary general Sayyid Hassan Nasrallah reportedly sent letters to eight Arab foreign ministries (Egypt, Syria, Lebanon, Palestine, Iraq, Yemen, Algeria, and Sudan) asking them to provide a list of their nationals in Israeli prisons.[38] Hizballah has also conditioned a prisoner swap on Israel handing over all of its maps to the minefields that it and its former proxy militia, the South Lebanon Army (SLA), laid during Israel's occupation of south Lebanon.

At this point, it is unclear if a prisoner exchange will occur and what its scope would be; however, Barak is reportedly leaning toward a prisoner exchange rather than risking a cross-border recovery operation.[39] In mid-December, a Lebanese newspaper owned by Lebanese Prime Minister Rafiq al-Hariri confirmed that the Israeli soldiers are alive and detailed an emerging two-stage prisoner swap deal.[40] Reportedly, negotiations have been conducted through at three least separate diplomatic channels (German, Austrian, and Russian),[41] but an agreement between Israel and Hezballah does not appear imminent at present.

Both the timing and nature of Hizballah's operation to capture the Israeli soldiers were unsurprising. Ever since Israel withdrew from south Lebanon without releasing all of its Lebanese prisoners, Hizballah had made freeing those prisoners one of its highest priorities. Accordingly, Israeli intelligence and military sources had issued repeated warnings that Hizballah planned to engage in military operations and possibly kidnap soldiers.[42]

---

[37] Fayez 'Abbas, "Demanding Arab Israelis in Exchange for the Kidnapped Soldiers," *Yediot Aharonot*, October 11, 2000.

[38] "Letters from Hizballah to the Egyptian Foreign Ministry and Seven Arab Countries Asking to Define the Number of Their Prisoners in Israel in Preparation for Their Swap," *al-Quds al-'Arabi*, December 28, 2000.

[39] Aluf Benn, Amos Harel, Amir Oren, and Amira Hess, "Barak in an Ultimatum to Arafat: A Calming Tomorrow or a Cessation of Negotiations," *Ha'aretz*, October 10, 2000.

[40] "The Israeli Prisoners Are Alive and a Swap Is Near," *al-Mustaqbal*, December 13, 2000.

[41] Oren Tivenbraun, "Israel Operated Three Channels to Negotiate the Release of the Captives," *Yediot Aharonot*, December 27, 2000.

[42] For instance, see Sharon Gal, "Security Source: Hizballah Is Planning an Attack at Har Dov [Sheba'a Farms]," *Ha'aretz*, September 25, 2000.

Regional Implications

Arab/Muslim Reactions

Growing scepticism over the stalled peace process, anger over Sharon's visit to al-Haram ash-Sharif/Temple Mount, and outrage at the number of Palestinians killed and wounded have fueled a strong reaction against Israel and to a lesser extent the United States throughout the Arab world. Pro-Palestinian demonstrations have taken place in most Arab countries, including those friendly to the United States, and in some non-Arab Muslim countries as well such as Iran, Pakistan, and Indonesia. Most Arab governments, dismayed by the turn of events, have walked a tight rope between supporting the Palestinian cause, condemning Israeli actions, and curbing popular outbursts that might jeopardize stability in their own countries. Gulf states, in particular, have been active in providing relief to Palestinians during the current crisis. Some hard line states and various Palestinian groups, however, have called for more stringent measures including dissolution of ties with Israel and the United States, termination of peace negotiations with Israel, a boycott of Israeli and U.S. products, and support for Palestinian military action against Israel.

Decisions reached at an October Arab League summit conference generally reflected the positions of more moderate Arab leaders, although attendees strongly criticized U.S. support for Israel. In its closing statement, the conference accused Israel of sole responsibility for the clashes, created funds to support families of Palestinian fighters and to help "preserve the Arab identity of Jerusalem" (see above), called for dispatching an international peacekeeping force to the occupied territories, and recommended that Arab states suspend participation in international conferences involving Israel and postpone any new steps toward normalizing relations with Israel. Finally, in what was probably an indirect warning to the United States, conferees vowed to break diplomatic relations with any country that moved its embassy to Jerusalem, although the statement did not mention the United States by name. As the fighting has continued in the aftermath of the October summit, however, even moderate Arab states have felt compelled to downgrade relations with Israel, while maintaining their support for the peace process. More militant leaders condemn any resumption of peace talks and urge that the intifadah continue until Palestinian goals are met.

Egypt, Jordan, and Mauritania

Two of the three Arab countries that have established full diplomatic relations with Israel have reduced the level of their diplomatic ties with Israel while maintaining formal diplomatic relations. On November 21, Egypt recalled its ambassador from Israel (only the second time it has done so since the 1979 Israeli-Egyptian peace treaty), after Israel bombarded the Gaza Strip in response to an attack on an Israeli school bus. On the same day, Jordanian Prime Minister Ali Abu Raghib announced that Jordan would defer sending its new ambassador-designate to Israel "until Israel ends its attacks and proves commitments toward the peace process." Distant Mauritania, more insulated from mainstream Arab reactions, said it would maintain existing diplomatic links with Israel but on November 22 a government spokesman denounced "the Israeli military escalation against the Palestinian people, in particular the bombing of civilians."

As fighting continued, there were further reactions in Egypt and Jordan at both the governmental and popular levels. On December 12, Egyptian President Husni Mubarak commented that citizens were justified in boycotting Israeli goods, but cautioned that they should consider carefully the effects of boycotting U.S. goods. Condemnation of Israel was widespread in Jordan, where a majority of the population is Palestinian and a strong Islamic movement exists. On December 5, a militant Islamic group claimed responsibility for an attack on an Israeli diplomat, leading to an Israeli decision to evacuate families of Israeli diplomats in Jordan. Both countries, however, continue to work with U.S. leaders in seeking a resumption of Israeli-Palestinian negotiations. In an editorial published on December 10, the Egyptian ambassador to the United States affirmed that "[t]he question before us is how, not whether, to resume the peace process."[43] More recently, Egypt and Jordan, along with Saudi Arabia, have reportedly lent their support to the general concept of a further peace proposal floated by President Clinton in late December.[44]

Morocco and Tunisia

Two other North African states, Morocco and Tunisia, suspended their ties with Israel in reaction to the intifadah. Both countries had established low level commercial relations with Israel in the aftermath of the 1993 Oslo agreement, and

[43] Nabil Fahmy, "Peace Is Still Possible in the Middle East,"*New York Times*, December 10, 2000.
[44] Jane Perlez, "Three Arab Leaders React Favorably To Mideast Plan,"*New York Times*, December 28, 2000.

Morocco under the late King Hassan II had long been a pioneer in facilitating Arab-Israeli contacts. The King of Morocco (Hassan and now his successor Muhammad VI) occupies a key position in the Muslim world as Chairman of the Jerusalem Committee of the 55-member Islamic Conference Organization. During the past year, an estimated 50,000 Israelis visited Morocco and 1,000 Moroccans, most of them from Morocco's Jewish community, visited Israel. It is not clear whether or not the closure of Israeli-Moroccan liaison offices will affect tourism between the two countries. Both Morocco and Tunisia, however, seem interested in pursuing Arab-Israeli peace efforts. A senior U.S. diplomat visited Tunisia in December to enlist its support, and former Israeli Prime Minister Shimon Peres visited Morocco on December 28 for discussions with King Muhammad on the peace process.

The Arabian Peninsula

Saudi Arabia

The leaders of Saudi Arabia have tried to balance their strategic and economic ties with the United States with their support for Palestinian positions, particularly regarding Jerusalem. Saudi statements have combined measured criticism of Israeli pressures on the United States with pleas for continued U.S. efforts to achieve a just peace. Shortly after the intifadah began, Crown Prince Abdullah warned that Saudi Arabia and other Arab countries would not "just watch with their hands tied" as Palestinian casualties mounted, and the Crown Prince later told a group of Islamic leaders that "I place particular emphasis on the United States because it has been following the development of the peace process since it was launched." Defense Minister Prince Sultan commented that "[w]e have no doubt that the United States wants peace in the region, but we ask it to change its methods with the Israelis in order to ensure a just and comprehensive solution."[45] In November 2000, Saudi Arabia agreed to attend a meeting of the Islamic Conference Organization in Qatar only on condition that Qatar sever its low level commercial ties with Israel, as Tunisia, Morocco, and Oman had done. So far, however, Saudi Arabia has made no move to use oil as a weapon to induce the United States or its allies to alter their policies on the Palestinian-Israeli conflict.

[45] David Butter, "Taking a lead," *Middle East Economic Digest*, December 1, 2000, p. 29.

Yemen

Neighboring Yemen has been unusually outspoken in condemning Israeli actions and upholding the Palestinian position. In the early stages of the intifadah, Yemeni President Ali Abdullah Salih said he wished Yemen had a common border with Palestinian territories to serve as a conduit for "holy warriors" and arms for the Palestinians and condemned the resolutions of the October 23 Arab summit as insufficient. In other statements he said Yemen supports peace but insists that Palestinians have the means of self-defense, expressed respect for America, but called for ending the Israeli occupation of Palestinian territory. Initial speculation that the bombing attack on the U.S.S. Cole in the Yemeni port of Aden on October 12, 2000 was linked to the Palestinian intifadah appear incorrect, as evidence has mounted that the attack had been planned some months earlier by terrorist groups targeting U.S. and allied military forces in the Persian Gulf region.[46]

Oman

On October 12, the generally pro-U.S. government of Oman told Israel to close its trade office in Oman's capital, Muscat. Oman also closed its representative office in Tel Aviv. The two countries exchanged trade offices in 1995.

Qatar

After several weeks of resisting Arab and Islamic pressure to close Israel's trade office, Qatar yielded on that issue when several of these countries threatened not to attend an Organization of Islamic Conference (OIC) meeting in Qatar on November 9, 2000. That office was opened in 1996, although Qatar never opened a reciprocal office in Israel. However, Qatar did not announce a complete severing of relations and Israeli and Qatari diplomats have since continued to meet at the margins of international meetings and conferences. Israeli diplomats say the trade office in Qatar is quietly still being allowed to operate at a reduced level, and Israel's trade office head, Eli Avidar, is still in Qatar. This could suggest that the state is trying to quietly allay U.S. concerns about Qatar's posture toward Israel without openly offending Qatar's Arab and Islamic allies.

---

[46] For further information, see CRS Report RS20721, *Terrorist Attack on USS Cole: Background and Issues for Congress*, by Raphael Perl and Ronald O'Rourke, November 1, 2000, and CRS Report RS20733, *Yemen: U.S. Relations, Assistance, and the U.S.S. Cole Bombing*, by Alfred B. Prados, November 20, 2000.

Iraq

At the outset of the intifadah, Iraq's President Saddam Husayn threatened Israel rhetorically and, in a symbolic gesture of support for the Palestinians, briefly moved a division of its Republican Guard westward toward Jordan. Yasser Arafat's PLO supported Iraq in the Gulf war, and many Palestinians have often seen Saddam as a hero in a longterm battle against Israel. U.S. Secretary of Defense Cohen said that the United States was watching the Iraqi troop movements closely, but the deployments did not appear to represent an intended military move outside Iraq's borders. Saddam has since urged the Palestinians to continue their uprising rather than agree to U.S.-sponsored attempts to end the violence.

Iraq has recently attempted to draw some implicit linkages between support for the Palestinians and Iraq's own struggle to weaken international sanctions imposed on it as a result of its 1990 invasion of Kuwait. Despite widespread concern about the plight of the Iraqi people under more than ten years of U.N. sanctions, in early November Iraq began shipping medicine and foodstuffs to the Palestinians, and has even used some of its scarce currency reserves to donate up to $10,000 to the family of each Palestinian killed in the violence.[47] On December 9, Iraq pledged to allocate about $880 million in oil revenues generated under its U.N.-sponsored "oil-for-food" program to Palestinian families. However, Iraq's oil revenues are deposited into a U.N. escrow account, and any donations from that account would have to receive U.N. Security Council approval. The United States is likely to oppose the donations on the grounds that the oil revenues are to be used for the relief of the Iraqi people alone, and not to further Iraqi political goals.

Iran

There are reports that Iran is encouraging its allies, including Hamas, Hizballah, Palestinian Islamic Jihad, and the Popular Front for the Liberation of Palestine-General Command, to continue the violence against Israel.[48] Iran's Islamic government has always opposed the peace process on the grounds that the Palestinians cannot hope to achieve a fair settlement with Israel, but Iran's President Mohammad Khatemi has said several times since taking office in August 1997 that Iran would not work to derail peace efforts. Nonetheless,

---

[47] Roni Shaked,"$10,000 per Shahid [Martyr]," *Yediot Aharonot*, December 13, 2000.

[48] "Iran, Palestinians Discuss How to Continue Unrest," *Reuters*, October 11, 2000.

hardline institutions in Iran have continued to provide material support to Palestinian rejectionist groups, according to official U.S. reports and statements, and Iran has publicly announced training maneuvers between its hardline security organs and anti-peace process groups. On December 15, Iran's Supreme Leader Ali Khamene'i, who is aligned with the hardline wing of Iran's regime, repeated an earlier statement that Israel "has no right to exist," and that it is "a cancerous tumor that should be uprooted from this region."[49]

CONGRESS AND THE AL-AQSA INTIFADAH

In the 106th Congress, Members introduced legislation stating that the Palestinian uprising was premeditated, initiated, and orchestrated by the Palestinian Authority (PA) and that the PA encouraged and incited the Palestinian people to attack the Israelis. H.Con.Res. 418 and H.Con.Res. 426 supported Israel's actions, and encouraged the U.S. Administration to oppose any anti-Israel resolutions in the United Nations and to persuade the Palestinians to negotiate a resolution. H.Con.Res. 426 passed the House on October 25, 2000, by a vote of 365 to 30, with 11 abstentions. H.R. 5522 proposed cutting foreign assistance to the Palestinians if the Palestinians did not stop the uprising. H.Res. 623 as introduced stated that the House of Representatives "denounces the abstention by the United States from voting on [U.N. Security Council] Resolution 1322" that "deplored" Israel's September 28 provocation in Jerusalem.

[49] "Iran's Leader Calls For Big Turnouts at Israel Protests," *Dow Jones Newswire*, December 15, 2000.

Chapter 4

THE PLO AND ITS FACTIONS

Kenneth Katzman

INTRODUCTION

During the current Palestinian uprising, several Palestinian factions apparently linked in varying degrees to the Palestine Liberation Organization (PLO) have used violence in an effort to force Israel to end its occupation of Palestinian territory. There is a debate over the degree to which PLO Chairman and Palestinian Authority President Yasir Arafat is willing and able to prevent anti-Israel violence by these factions. This report will be updated to reflect regional developments.

BACKGROUND ON THE PLO AND YASIR ARAFAT

Yasir Arafat was born Mohammad Abd Ar-Raouf on August 24, 1929, in Jerusalem. While studying in Egypt in 1944, he founded the League of Palestinian Students, and later earned an engineering degree from King Fuad University in Egypt. Arafat served in the Egyptian army as a demolition specialist during the 1956 Suez war between Egypt and Britain, France, and Israel. In 1957, Arafat helped founded the Fatah (Conquest) guerrilla organization, also known as the Palestine National Liberation Movement. The Palestine Liberation Organization (PLO) was formally established in 1964, and Fatah joined it in 1968, immediately becoming its dominant organization. In 1969, Arafat was named PLO executive chairman. The Palestine National Council (PNC) is the highest decisionmaking body of the PLO, and is considered to be the "parliament"[1] of all Palestinians inside and outside the occupied territories. The PNC "sets PLO policies," according to the website of the Permanent Observer Mission of Palestine to the United Nations.[2] Arafat is also known as Abu Amar.

Neither the PLO as a whole, nor the Fatah movement, has been named by the State Department as a Foreign Terrorist Organization (FTO). The PLO formally renounced the use of terrorism in 1988 and committed itself to peace with Israel in several agreements since 1993.[3] (The FTO list is maintained by the State Department under the Anti-Terrorism and Effective Death Penalty Act of 1996, P.L. 104-132, and the State Department can add or delete a group from that list at any time.)

A number of different groups have been part of the PLO coalition; these groups have their own prominent founders and their own organizational structures. Some of the leaders of these PLO constituent groups have, at times, been rivals or competitors of Arafat for support among Palestinians. Several are considered "rejectionist" groups, having opposed the September 13, 1993 Israel-PLO mutual recognition and subsequent Israeli-Palestinian interim agreements. Major groups, apart from Fatah, have included:

- the Popular Front for the Liberation of Palestine (PFLP)**Error! Bookmark not defined.**, a Marxist group which suspended its participation in the PLO after the 1993 Israel-Palestinian Declaration of Principles (Israel-PLO mutual recognition, agreement to seek a peaceful settlement). It was founded by George Habash.
- the Popular Front for the Liberation of Palestine-General Command (PFLP-GC), led by Ahmad Jibril, a Damascus based faction that is politically close to Syria. It also suspended its participation in the PLO.
- The Democratic Front for the Liberation of Palestine (DFLP), led by Nayif Hawatmeh, also a Marxist organization that resumed participation in the PLO in 1999.

---

[1] Although the PLO describes the PNC as a parliament, the PNC should not be confused with the Palestine Legislative Council (PLC), the legislature of the Palestinian Authority, which represents only the residents of the West Bank and Gaza. Elections for the PLC were held in January 1996.

[2] The website is located at: [http://www.palestine-un.org].

[3] For further information on the Israeli-Palestinian peace process, see CRS Issue Brief IB92052, *Palestinians and Middle East Peace: Issues for the United States*, and CRS Issue Brief IB91137, *The Middle East Peace Talks*.

- the Palestine Liberation Front (PLF), a small group, led by Abu Abbas, that is still participating in the PLO.

Three of these groups – the PFLP, the PFLP-GC, and the PLF – have claimed responsibility for acts of terrorism since the 1993 Declaration of Principles and are named by the State Department as FTO's.[4] The DFLP was named as an FTO when the first FTO list was issued in October 1997, but, because of a degree of reconciliation with Arafat and apparent acceptance of eventual peace with Israel, it was dropped when the list was revised in October 1999.

Minor groups in the PLO coalition – none of which is named as an FTO – are: As-Saiqa, a pro-Syrian faction not currently participating in the PLO; the Arab Liberation Front, a pro-Iraqi faction that is participating in the PLO; the Popular Struggle Front, which is participating in the PLO; the People's Party, formerly called the Palestinian Communist Party and which is participating in the PLO; and the Democratic Union, commonly known by its initials "FIDA," a splinter faction of the DFLP which is participating in the PLO.

The PLO's Islamist Rivals: Hamas and Palestinian Islamic Jihad

Most of the anti-Israel violence since the 1993 Declaration of Principles and during the current Palestinian uprising has been conducted by Islamist groups – notably Hamas and Palestinian Islamic Jihad (PIJ). Both of these groups are named as FTO's. Neither has ever been part of the PLO coalition, and the two groups have been widely considered opponents of Arafat and the PLO. Hamas and PIJ reject the PLO's secular ideology and stated commitment to reaching a peace deal with Israel. On the other hand, Arafat and the two Islamist groups have occasionally sought to forge closer ties to each other. In June 2002, Arafat reportedly offered the two organizations seats in the PA cabinet, but they both refused, saying they could not serve in a government that is committed to reaching a peace deal with Israel.

[4] These groups, as well as other Palestinian groups such as Hamas and Palestinian Islamic Jihad, are discussed in greater depth in CRS Report RL31119, *Terrorism: Near Eastern Groups and State Sponsors, 2002*. The penalties for being named an FTO are discussed in that report.

MAJOR PLO GROUPS AND FACTIONS INVOLVED IN THE UPRISING

During the current Palestinian uprising that began in September 2000, violence and terrorism against Israelis have been conducted not only by Hamas and PIJ, but also by factions related to the PLO, and Fatah in particular. This development has shifted the focus of the debate over the PLO somewhat. Previously, U.S. official statements and reports on PLO compliance with its commitments to Israel, which are submitted to Congress every six months in reports pursuant to Title VIII of P.L. 101-246, the PLO Commitments Compliance Act, primarily assessed Arafat's willingness and ability to constrain terrorist activities by his rivals, Hamas and PIJ. In contrast, much of the current U.S. discussion of Arafat's goals and motives focuses on his willingness and ability to prevent anti-Israel violence and terrorism by PLO/Fatah-related factions that have traditionally been considered his allies or subordinates. Some of these factions, particularly the Al Aqsa Martyrs Brigades, are increasingly using suicide tactics that traditionally have been characteristic of Hamas and PIJ.

There are four major PLO-related organizations and factions that have attracted recent Administration and congressional interest for their relatively high level of involvement in anti-Israel violence during the current uprising. They are: Fatah itself, Arafat's key power base within the PLO; Force-17, a PLO security service; and two Fatah offshoots – the Tanzim (Arabic word for "organization"), and the Al Aqsa Martyrs Brigades. The Al Aqsa Martyrs Brigades was designated an FTO on March 27, 2002; Fatah, Force 17, and the Tanzim have not been designated as FTO's.

The Administration's PLO compliance report of May 7, 2002, covering the period June 16, 2001 to December 15, 2001, and the State Department report on international terrorism for 2001 (*Patterns of Global Terrorism 2001*, released May 21, 2002) discuss the involvement of PLO-related groups factions in anti-Israel violence. The PLO compliance report states that "...available evidence indicates that elements with varying degrees of affiliation with the PLO, specifically the Al Aqsa Martyrs Brigade, Tanzim, Force 17, and members of other security forces, were frequently involved in acts of violence against Israelis." The report adds that, "While there is no conclusive evidence that these elements acted with the prior approval and encouragement of the PLO and PA (Palestinian Authority) leadership, it is clear that these armed elements were not disciplined." The *Patterns of Global Terrorism* report cited above (P.54) states that members of the Tanzim and the Al Aqsa Martyrs Brigade conducted attacks against Israeli targets in 2001. The Administration's previous report on PLO compliance, which covered the period December 15, 2000 - June 15, 2001, said that "some elements of the PA security forces and Chairman Arafat's Fatah faction within the PLO were deeply involved in the violence" against Israelis. That report added that "Mid-level PA and Fatah officials, including of the Tanzim, have publicly advocated violence."

The following is background on the four PLO-related groups and factions.

Fatah

Fatah, as noted above, is Arafat's core power base within the PLO, and the faction over which Arafat, a key Fatah founder, presumably has the most control. Fatah's founders were, like Arafat, Palestinians students in Egypt during the 1950s. Upon completing their studies, many, including Arafat, went to the Persian Gulf states to avoid the politically repressive atmosphere of Egypt under Gamal Abd al-Nasser. Fatah's founders emphasized their own Palestinian nationalist ideology more than Nasser's Arab nationalist ideology and conducted cross-border guerrilla activity against Israel from Jordan and Lebanon. According to the Palestinian U.N. website, in the mid 1970s (after the October 1973 Arab-Israeli war) Fatah led the "pragmatic transition toward engagement in a political settlement" with Israel.

Force 17

Force 17 was formed in the early 1970s as a personal security force for Arafat and other PLO leaders. Force 17 members were involved in attacks on Israeli targets in the early 1980s and it claimed responsibility for killing three Israelis in Cyprus in 1985. In 1994, when the PA was established, Force 17 was merged into the official PA security apparatus and technically ceased to exist, although some PA security officials apparently continue to identify themselves as Force 17 members. It is widely presumed that Arafat has a degree of control over Force 17 because it is part of the PA security structure. Those members of Force 17 who are allegedly involved in violence against Israel do not appear to have a clearly identifiable leadership apart from Arafat.

The Tanzim

The Tanzim militia is widely considered an armed offshoot of Fatah, but it has developed its own structure and leadership. For that reason, Arafat's influence over the Tanzim is probably less extensive than within Fatah or Force 17. The acknowledged head of the Tanzim is Marwan Barghouti, who is the secretary-general of Fatah in the West Bank and, according to some accounts, is increasingly viewed as a potential successor to Arafat.[5] At the same time, Barghouti has publicly praised Arafat as an effective Palestinian leader and has said, in editorials written in U.S. newspapers, that Palestinian violence is for the purpose only of ending Israel's occupation of Palestinian territories, and not to destroy Israel. The precise relationship between Arafat and Barghouti is not known. Barghouti says he "still seek[s] peaceful coexistence between the equal and independent countries of Israel and Palestine based on full withdrawal from Palestinian territories occupied in 1967 and a just resolution to the plight of Palestinian refugees pursuant to U.N. resolutions."[6] Barghouti, who is about 42 years old, has been incarcerated by Israel since Israeli forces arrested him in mid-April 2002 during their military incursion into the Palestinian territories. Barghouti was a student activist at Bir Zeit University in the 1980s, and was imprisoned by Israel for six years (1982-1988) for Fatah activities. He was deported to Jordan in 1988 and returned to the West Bank in 1994 under the terms of the Oslo accords.

The Tanzim militia was established in 1995 by Arafat and the Fatah leadership as a paramilitary force intended to offset the power of the Palestinian Islamist groups, particularly Hamas and PIJ. Fatah's decision to form the Tanzim was apparently motivated, at least in part, by armed confrontations in 1994 between PA security forces and members of Hamas. The Tanzim is also a grass roots organization that operates at the community level and, by taking a hardline position toward Israel, it has helped siphon Palestinian support from the Islamist groups to the PA and PLO leadership. Since the latest Palestinian uprising began, it has reportedly been involved in firing on Israeli soldiers during Palestinian demonstrations, and some mortar attacks on Israeli settlements. According to available information, the Tanzim has not conducted suicide bombings against Israelis, perhaps explaining why it has not been designated an FTO.

---

[5] Kifner, John. As Arafat Critics Close In, Deputies Vie in the Wings. *New York Times*, May 21, 2002.

[6] Barghouti, Marwan. Want Security? End the Occupation. *Morning Star*, January 31, 2002.

Al Aqsa Martyrs Brigades

Of the PLO-related organizations discussed in this section, the Al Aqsa Martyrs Brigades, is the only one named as an FTO. It has been so designated on the grounds that it has claimed responsibility for carrying out suicide bombings against Israeli civilians. The Brigades appears to have sprung up spontaneously, after the start of the latest Palestinian uprising, reportedly formed by Tanzim or other Fatah activists who believe in a more aggressive approach to forcing Israel to end its occupation. Al Aqsa Martyrs Brigades members say they do not share the ideology of Hamas and PIJ, which purport to seek Israel's destruction. Brigades members say they are interested in a peace process as long as a final settlement results in Israel's full withdrawal from the occupied territories and provides for the right of return of Palestinian refugees.[7]

The Al Aqsa Martyrs Brigades does not have a well defined structure and, of the factions discussed in this section, is the one over which Arafat would appear to have the least political control. There is no firm evidence that Arafat selected any leaders or commanders of the Brigades or specifically authorized its formation. According to some press reports, commanders of the Brigades frequently take issue with Arafat, and Arafat's representatives are constantly debating Palestinian strategy and tactics with the Brigades.[8] On the other hand, some point to statements by Martyrs Brigades commanders and PA officials as supporting the argument that the Brigades are under Arafat's control. One Brigades commander told a journalist in March 2002 that "Our group is an integral part of Fatah."[9] Other analysts quote a senior Fatah leader, Hussein al-Sheikh, as saying that Fatah controls the Brigades "to one extent or another."

CONCLUSIONS AND PROSPECTS

It is not possible from publicly available information to determine the exact extent to which Arafat is able to or has sought to control Palestinian factions that use violence. During its incursion into the West Bank in April 2002, Israel claimed to have captured Palestinian documents purporting to demonstrate Arafat's backing for terrorism by some of these factions. The Palestinians say that

---

[7] Biedermann, Ferry. Secular and Deadly: The Rise of the Martyrs Brigades. Salon.com, March 19, 2002.

[8] Williams, Daniel. A Magnet for Palestinian 'Martyrs;' Al Aqsa Brigades Lead New Wave of Attacks on Israeli Civilians. *Washington Post*, March 7, 2002.

[9] Kalman, Matthew. Terrorist Says Orders Come From Arafat. *USA Today*, March 14, 2002.

the documents are either forged or have been misrepresented by Israel. U.S. government agencies have not made a public assessment of these documents to date. Arafat has denounced suicide terrorism against Israel after terrorist events, and the U.S. government reports cited above do not publicly corroborate or support Israeli allegations that Arafat himself has authorized acts of terrorism against Israelis. On the other hand, U.S. officials, including President Bush, have repeatedly criticized Arafat since January 2002 for failing to do all he could to prevent anti-Israel violence. Those who believe Arafat is actively supporting violence and terrorism against Israel assert that Arafat feels that violence can be a useful tactic in forcing concessions from Israel, or perhaps even precipitating Israel's demise. Others argue that terrorist acts are counterproductive for Arafat since they undercut his credibility as a negotiating partner.

Some in Congress believe that the United States should, among other steps, specifically sanction the PLO and some of its factions. Section 4 of H.R. 1795, the Middle East Peace Commitments Act of 2001, introduced by Representative Ackerman, Representative Gilman, and Representative Lantos on May 10, 2001, directs the President to "designate the PLO, or one or more of its constituent groups (including Fatah and Tanzim) or groups operating as arms of the Palestinian Authority (including Force 17)" as an FTO. A companion bill, S. 1409, was introduced in the Senate by Senator McConnell on September 6, 2001. Opponents of the legislation believe that naming Fatah, the Tanzim, or Force 17 as terrorist groups would indicate that the United States no longer views Arafat as a legitimate Palestinian peace interlocutor, and damage prospects for a peaceful solution to the violence.

Chapter 5

MIDDLE EAST PEACE: THE REFUGEE ISSUE

Clyde Mark and Kenneth Katzman

BACKGROUND[1]

As a result of the 1948-1949 war in Palestine between the Jews and Arabs, many Palestinian Arabs fled Jewish controlled areas and became refugees. The number of refugees in 1948-1949 is in dispute: Israeli sources estimate between 500,000 and 700,000; Arab sources estimate the number between 700,000 and one million; and the United Nations conciliation Commission placed the number at 726,000 in its 1949 report. Why the Arabs fled also is in dispute. Many Israelis claim the Arabs left their homes at the urging of Arab leaders to clear the battlefields for the Arab attacks on the Jews. Arabs claim the Palestinians left because they were driven out by the Israelis or because they feared for their lives.

The United Nations created the U.N. Relief for Palestine Refugees in October 1949, later renamed the U.N. Relief and Works Agency (UNRWA), to provide shelter, food, clothing, medical treatment, and education and training for the Palestinian refugees. Not all of the three and one half million Palestinians registered with UNRWA receive all the benefits; some receive only educational assistance or medical services, others may receive shelter only, or food and

---

[1] For general background on the refugee issue, see Morris, Benny. *The Birth of the Palestine Refugee Problem*. New York, Cambridge University Press, 1987, 380 p Khouri, Fred J. *The Arab-Israeli Dilemma.* Second edition, New York, Syracuse University Press, 1976. 466 p. Chapter VI, pps. 123-181. Peretz, Don. *The Palestine Arab Refugee Problem*. Santa Monica, California, Rand Corp., 1969. 74 p.

shelter. UNRWA's budget for FY2000 is $300.9 million, of which the United States will contribute about $80 million. As of June 30, 1999, UNRWA registered refugees were located as shown in Table 1.

Table 1. Location of Registered Refugees (As of June 30, 1999)

Location	Total Registered	Total in Camps	Number Camps
Jordan	1,512,742	274,816	10
Lebanon	370,144	204,999	12
Syria	374,521	109,315	10
West Bank	569,741	153,380	19
Gaza Strip	798,444	437,650	8
Totals	3,625,592	1,180,160	59

Source: Report of the Commissioner-General of the United Nations Relief and Works Agency for Palestinian Refugees in the Near East. July 1, 1998-June 30, 1999, A/54/13, General Assembly official records, 54th session.

During the 1967 war, another 325,000 Arabs fled the fighting, some of whom were first time refugees and others who had been refugees from the 1948-1949 conflict. The great majority of the 1967 refugees went to Jordan. They are not registered with UNRWA.

CURRENT STATUS OF PALESTINIAN ARAB REFUGEES

Palestinian Arabs living in the West Bank and Gaza areas under Palestinian Authority control enjoy many rights of Palestinian citizenship, such as voting in the 1996 legislative council and presidential elections, Palestine passports, due process under a Palestinian judicial system, and others. Jordan granted citizenship to the Palestinians living in Jordan and the West Bank in 1950. Palestinian refugees living in Syria, Lebanon, Iraq, Egypt, or other Arab countries have not been granted citizenship in their country of residence. The Palestinians who remained in areas that became the state of Israel became Israeli citizens, although their movement, occupation, housing, and other aspects of life remained restricted under military rule until 1966, and some de facto limitations still apply in schooling, housing, jobs, and business opportunities.

The "Right of Return"

Paragraph 11 of United Nations General Assembly Resolution 194 of December 11, 1949, states that the United Nations:

"Resolves that the refugees wishing to return to their homes and live at peace with their neighbours should be permitted to do so at the earliest practicable date, and that compensation should be paid for the property of those choosing not to return and for loss of or damage to property which, under principles of international law or in equity, should be made good by the Governments or authorities responsible..."

Another U.N. Resolution dealt with the refugees from the 1967 war. Operative paragraph one of U.N. Security Council Resolution 237 (1967), passed unanimously on June 14, 1967, called upon Israel "...to facilitate the return of those inhabitants who have fled the areas since the outbreak of hostilities..."

The Palestinians maintain that the refugees must be given the choice of repatriation or compensation, that those choosing repatriation must be allowed to return to the homes, shops, and farms they left in 1948-1949 or 1967, and that Israel, in Arab opinion the party responsible for the refugee flight, must pay the compensation to the individual refugees. Israel rejects the refugees' right to return. Israel maintains that it is not responsible for the Arab refugees leaving their homes in 19489-1949 or 1967, that it has no assurance that the refugees are willing to live in peace with the Israelis, and that the international community should be responsible for paying compensation.

The Refugee Issue in Current Negotiations

Article V, Paragraph 3 of the Israel-Palestine Liberation Organization Declaration of Principles, signed on September 13, 1993, states that Israel and the Palestinians will address the Palestinian refugee issue in the permanent status negotiations.[2] Israel and the Palestinians held one negotiating session in May 1996, resumed full negotiations on September 13, 1999, and are supposed to complete talks by September 13, 2000. It is not clear if the parties will meet the September deadline. There are several aspects of the refugee issue to be resolved: (1) Should the refugees be offered a choice of returning to the homes they left or receiving compensation for their lost property, as called for in U.N. Resolution 194? (2) If refugees are allowed to return to their homes, how many should return,

---

[2] For general information on the peace process, see CRS Issue Brief 91137, *Middle East Peace Talks*, updated periodically.

which ones, and who will select those returning? (3) If refugees are to be compensated for their lost property, will the compensation be calculated at the value of the property at the time it was abandoned or at today's value, and will the compensation be paid to individuals or to a collective body, such as the Palestine Liberation organization (PLO) or a Palestinian state? (4) Who will pay the compensation, Israel or the international community? (5) Where will the refugees be settled if they do not return to the homes they abandoned?

The Refugee Working Group, one of five multilateral groups that emerged from the Madrid process in 1991,[3] in its sporadic meetings has focused on humanitarian aspects of the refugee issue, such as family reunification or improving current living conditions. The more difficult questions – right of return, resettlement location and funding, compensation – are left to the bilateral negotiations between Israel and the Palestinians and to the regional negotiations among Jordan, Egypt, Israel, and the Palestinians. Israel and the Palestinians have addressed the refugee issue in the bilateral talks, but without any announced success. No regional negotiations have been held.

U.S. Policy toward the Refugees

The United States votes for UNGA Resolution 194 that included paragraph 11 calling for compensation or repatriation. The United States voted for U.N. Security Council Resolution 242 of November 1967 that called for a just settlement of the refugees problem (paragraph 2), and for UNSC Resolution 237 that called for the return of the 1967 refugees. The United States also votes for and has supported UNRWA, providing between one-quarter and one-third of UNRWA's annual budget.

The prevailing view in the United States from 1948 to 1967 was that the Palestinians primarily were refugees, not a nation or participants in the peace process. As the PLO and other Palestinian military organizations became active in the wake of the 1967 conflict, this perception shifted and some in the United States stopped seeing the Palestinians only as refugees, and began seeing them as terrorists (or occasionally as guerrilla fighters). In 1977, President Carter broadened the perception of the Palestinians when he said the Palestinians deserved a homeland,[4] and in 1978, he reinforced the Palestinian national image

[3] Se CRS Report RL30311, *Middle East: The Multilateral Peace Talks*, May 16, 2000.

[4] March 16, 1977 town meeting in Clinton, Massachusetts, U.S. President. *Public Papers of the Presidents of the United States*. Jimmy Carter, 1977. Book I. Washington, U.S. Gov't. Print. Off., 1977. p. 387.

when he said that they should participate in the peace process.[5] President Reagan said in September 1982 that the Palestinians were more than a refugee issue and had legitimate rights,[6] and the Reagan Administration opened a dialogue with the PLO in December 1988.[7] President Bush included the Palestinians as participants in the peace process begun at Madrid in 1991, although the Palestinians were seated with the Jordanian delegation at Israeli insistence. Israel and the United States recognized the PLO as a result of the 1993 Oslo process.[8]

President Clinton raised Israeli ire on July 1, 1999, when he said that the Palestinians should be free to live wherever they wanted, a statement considered by many Israelis and pro-Israel supporters to endorse the Palestinian contention that they are entitled to compensation or repatriation, as envisioned in U.N. Resolution 194. Israeli prime Minister Ehud Barak said the Clinton statement was "unacceptable." On July 2, 1 Department of State spokesman explained that U.S. policy had not changed, and that the United States continued to favor a resolution of the refugee problem derived from direct negotiations between the parties.[9]

Congressional Interest

Congress may focus on two aspects of the refugee problem; first, a resolution of the refugee issue as an integral part of peace between the Palestinians and Israelis, and second, possible requests for U.S. participation in financing the resettlement and compensation of the refugees.

Options for Resolving the Refugee Problem

The prevailing Israeli opinion appears to be that the Palestinian refugees should be settled in the lands where they now reside. Israelis differ over the

[5] Question and answer session January 6, 1978. U.S. Presidents. *Public Papers of the Presidents of the United States*. Jimmy Carter, 1978. Book I. Washington, U.S. Gov't. Print. Off., 1979. p. 44.

[6] Address to the nation, September 1, 1982. U.S. Presidents. *Public Papers of the Presidents of the United States,* Ronald Reagan, 1982. Book II. Washington, U.S. Gov't. Print. Off., 1983. Pp. 1094, 1095.

[7] Statement issued by the White House, December 14, 1988. U.S. Presidents. *Public Papers of the Presidents of the United States*, Ronald Reagan, 1988-1989. Book II. Washington, U.S. Gov't. Print. Off., 1991. p. 1627-1628.

[8] Remarks, September 10, 1993. U.S. Presidents. *Public Papers of the Presidents of the United States,* William J. Clinton, 1993. Book II. Washington, U.S. Gov't. Print. Off., 1994. p. 1464.

[9] Press conference of Presidents Mubarak and Clinton, the White House, July 1, 1999. Press Briefing, Department of State, July 2, 1999. Kurtzman, Daniel, "Clinton Remarks Decried by Israel Supporters," *Jewish Telegraphic Agency*, July 8, 1999.

Palestinians' right to migrate to a Palestinian state or entity. Some Israelis concede the Palestinians' right to move freely among the Arab states, including a Palestinian state. Other Israelis maintain that Palestinians currently outside the West Bank and the Gaza Strip should not be allowed to migrate to these territories, or a Palestinian state because these Israelis fear than an overpopulated Palestine will become a threat to Israel.

It appears highly unlikely that Israel would accept any resolution that involves a significant number of Palestinian Arabs returning to the properties they left in 1948-1949 that are now within Israel's boundaries. Many of the homes and villages abandoned by the Palestinians were occupied by Jewish immigrants. Also, Israel destroyed an estimated 400 Arab villages, so there may not be anything to which some of the Palestinians may return. It is highly unlikely that Israel would agree to pay any significant amounts of compensation to the refugees. At this point, it is possible, but not probable, that Israel would accept a token number of Palestinian refugees under the rubric of family reunification (but not the "right of return") or pay a token amount of compensation as gestures toward the peace process.

On November 21, 1999, a labor party Knesset member proposed that Israel absorb 100,000 Palestinian refugees as a gesture toward the peace process, but Prime Minister Barak dismissed the proposal and repeated that Israel would accept no Palestinian refugees.[10] In the past, Israel has suggested that the Arab states were responsible for the refugee problem, and therefore the Arab states and the international community are responsible for compensation and settling the refugees. Israel might agree with any international scheme to resolve the refugee problem providing that the refugees did not settle in Israel, Israel did not have to pay the compensation, and the plan did not imply any Israeli responsibility for causing the refugee problem in the first place.

It is equally unlikely that some of the Arab states, Lebanon in particular, would accept a resolution that entailed granting citizenship to the Palestinian refugees resident in their countries. In Lebanon's case, the addition of 370,000 Sunni Muslims would unbalance the carefully arranged governmental structure that is based on a confessional balance among Christians, Sunni Muslims, Shia Muslims, and Druze. Iraq, Syria, Libya, Saudi Arabia, and other Arab countries have been suggested as final homes for many of the refugees, particularly those in Lebanon. Many observers guess that most of the million plus Palestinians living in Jordan and already enjoying Jordanian citizenship will remain where and as

[10] MP Urges Israel Take 100,000 Palestinian Refugees," *Reuters*, November 21, 1999. Goldin, Megan, "Barak Rules Out Return of Palestinian Refugees," *Reuters,* November 29, 1999.

they are, but with an internationally financed effort to eliminate the refugee camps and move the camp dwellers into Jordanian society. Similarly, the 375,000 Palestinians in Syria could become Syrian citizens and be integrated into the society, but Syrian Government reaction to such a proposal is unclear.

Observers have suggested that some Palestinian refugees could be settled in countries outside the Middle East, such as Canada, the United States, or Australia, but no concrete proposals along these lines have been offered to date.

Chapter 6

THE MIDDLE EAST PEACE TALKS

Carol Migdalovitz

INTRODUCTION

The end of the Cold War, the decline of the Soviet Union, and the U.S.-led victory in the Gulf war facilitated the beginning of a new peace process in 1991. Israel and the Palestinians discussed a 5-year period of interim self-rule leading to a final settlement. Israel and Syria discussed Israeli withdrawal from the Golan Heights in exchange for peace. Israel and Jordan discussed relations. Israel and Lebanon focused on Israel's withdrawal from its self-declared security zone in south Lebanon and reciprocal Lebanese actions.

On September 13, 1993, Israel and the Palestine Liberation Organization (PLO) signed a Declaration of Principles (DOP), providing for Palestinian empowerment and some territorial control. Israel and Jordan signed a peace treaty agenda on September 14, 1993; Prime Minister Rabin and King Hussein affirmed the end of the state of belligerency between Israel and Jordan on July 25; a Peace Treaty was signed on October 26, 1994. Israel and the Palestinians signed an Interim Self-Rule in the West Bank/Oslo II accord on September 28, 1995. Israel continued implementing it despite the November 4 assassination of Prime Minister Rabin.

Israel suspended talks with Syria after terror attacks in February/March 1996. They resumed in December 1999, but were "post-poned indefinitely" after January 2000.

A January 1997 protocol produced Israeli redeployment from Hebron. In 1998, the United States intensively mediated. An October 15-23 summit resulted in the Wye River Memorandum on implementation of earlier agreements. The Israeli cabinet froze implementation on December 20.

On September 4, 1999, Israeli Prime Minister Barak and Palestinian leader Arafat signed the Sharm al-Shaykh Memorandum on implementing Wye. Israel withdrew from south Lebanon on May 24, 2000. From July 11-24, President Clinton convened a summit with Israeli and Palestinian leaders at Camp David to reach a framework accord, but they did not succeed. A Palestinian uprising or *intifadah* began in September and continues. On December 23, President Clinton presented bridging proposals.

Ariel Sharon was elected Prime Minister of Israel on February 6, 2001. He said that the results of Camp David and subsequent talks were null and void. The international war against terrorism after September 11, 2001 prompted renewed U.S. focus on ending the violence and resuming the peace process. Yet the situation degenerated with suicide bombings and countermeasures. On June 24, 2002, President Bush declared, "peace requires new and different Palestinian leadership so that a Palestinian state can be born." The United States developed a "road map" to Palestinian statehood with the U.N., European Union, and Russia (the Quartet) and will present it when a new Palestinian government is in place.

Congress is interested in the peace talks because of its oversight role in the conduct of U.S. foreign policy, its support for Israel, and keen constituent interest. It is concerned about U.S. financial and other commitments and Palestinian fulfillment of commitments. Congress has appropriated aid for the West Bank and Gaza, with conditions intended to ensure Palestinian compliance with agreements with Israel. Congress repeatedly endorsed Jerusalem as the undivided capital of Israel, and many Members seek sanctions on the PLO and PA.

MOST RECENT DEVELOPMENTS

On March 14, President Bush declared that the road map (or peace process developed by the United States, U.N., European Union, and Russia – "the Quartet") would be given to the Palestinians and the Israelis "immediately upon confirmation" of a prime minister "of real authority." He also said that he would "expect and welcome contributions from Israel and the Palestinians to this document." On March 19, a State Department spokesman explained that the President would work with the parties on how to implement the road map. On March 31, National Security Advisor Rice indicated that the road map was not open to renegotiation. Israeli officials maintain that the road map is a sequential process in which the first stage or precondition for others is a cessation of violence. Foreign Minister Shalom said that Israel will respond favorably if the road map is identical to the vision of President Bush's June 24, 2002 speech (see below). The U.N., Europeans, and Palestinians regard the road map as a simultaneous process, with actions required by both sides at the same time. The Palestinians seek its immediate publication and implementation without changes. On April 4, Secretary of State Powell said that the road map would be unveiled "as it is" when a new Palestinian government takes office, but it would not be imposed. On April 6, the Chief of the Israeli Prime Minister's office said that Israel would submit 15 reservations on the road map. If a refusal of proposed changes could jeopardize Israel's security, then it would not accept the map. Islamic Jihad claimed responsibility for a March 30 suicide bombing that wounded 49 people in Netanya.

BACKGROUND AND ANALYSIS

Since the founding of Israel, Arab-Israeli conflict marked every decade until the 1990s. With each clash, issues separating the parties multiplied and became more intractable. The creation of the State of Israel in 1948 provided a home for the Jewish people, but the ensuing conflict made refugees of thousands of Arab residents of the formerly British Palestine, with consequences troubling for Arabs and Israelis alike. The 1967 war ended with Israel occupying territory of Egypt, Jordan, and Syria. Egypt and Syria fought the 1973 war, in part, to regain their lands. In 1982, Israel invaded southern Lebanon to prevent terrorist incursions; it withdrew in 1985, retaining control of a 9-mile "security zone" over which Lebanon seeks to reclaim. Middle East peace has been a U.S. and international diplomatic goal throughout the years of conflict. The 1978 Camp David talks, the only previous direct Arab-Israeli negotiations, brought about the 1979 Israel-Egypt Peace Treaty.

Changed International and Regional Scenes

At the height of the crisis he provoked in 1990, Iraqi President Saddam Husayn offered to withdraw from Kuwait if Israel withdrew from Arab territories it occupied. The United States and others denied a linkage, but on the day after the Gulf war began, January 18, 1991, President Bush declared, "When all this is over, we want to be the healers ...." On March 6, he defined U.S. postwar goals to include finding solutions to the Arab-Israeli conflict and the Lebanon situation, and sent Secretary of State Baker to the Middle East to organize a conference. The end of the Cold War and the decline of the Soviet Union aided him. During the Gulf war, the Soviets did not use their U.N. veto to prevent action and banned arms exports to Iraq. They needed Western aid and agreed with U.S. initiatives. They also were unable to continue diplomatic, military, and financial aid to Iraq, Syria, and the Palestine Liberation Organization (PLO). The failed August 1991 Moscow coup sidelined hard-liners. U.S. policymakers no longer viewed the Soviet Union as obstructionist and sought it to cosponsor of a peace conference.

Arab states, whose unity was damaged in the Gulf war, recognized the United States as the remaining superpower. Egypt, Syria, and the Gulf states (Saudi Arabia, Kuwait, Bahrain, the United Arab Emirates, Qatar, Oman) joined the anti-Iraq coalition. Gulf regimes depend on U.S. and allied military might. Since Camp David, Egypt has been a U.S. ally and the second largest recipient of U.S. foreign aid. Syria, opposed to Saddam Husayn and seeking benefactors, sent troops to defend Saudi Arabia. The PLO and Jordan, however, were sympathetic to Iraq and debilitated by the choice. The Gulf states ended aid for Jordan and the PLO as Palestinians fled the Gulf, inundating Jordan. European and other sympathy for the Palestinian cause eroded temporarily as Iraqi missiles hit Israeli civilian sites. Meanwhile, in the West Bank and Gaza, moderates argued for negotiations to ease the plight of the people. Thus, each party to the peace conference sought U.S. support: Egypt as a consequence of Camp David; Syria to replace lost Soviet patronage; Jordan to reclaim lost goodwill, aid, and trade; the Palestinians for some gain after years of loss; Israel because of its dependence on external, especially U.S., aid and resources.

Role of the United States

On March 6, 1991, President Bush outlined a framework for peace: grounded in U.N. Security Council Resolutions 242 and 338 and the principle of "territory for peace," providing for Israel's security and recognition of Palestinian political rights. Secretary of State Baker avoided declaring U.S. positions, but provided Israel, Syria, Lebanon, and the Palestinians non-binding letters of assurance that have not been released officially. He reportedly accepted Israel's view that 242 is subject to interpretation, stated that the United States would not support creation of an independent Palestinian state, and assured Israel that the United States would give "considerable weight" to Israel's view that the Golan Heights are important to its security. He reportedly assured Syria that the United States believes 242 applies to all fronts and gave Lebanon a commitment to its territorial integrity within its internationally recognized borders. He told the Palestinians that the United States wanted their legitimate political rights and opposed Israel's annexation of East Jerusalem.

President Clinton said that only the region's leaders can make peace, and vowed to be their partner. In February 1993, Secretary of State Christopher defined full partner as an intermediary or an honest broker, to "probe positions, clarify responses, help define common ground, offer what may be bridging ideas." With the Hebron Protocol of 1997, the United States became an indispensable party to Israeli-Palestinian talks. Clinton mediated the October 1998 Wye River Memorandum, and the United States undertook to coordinate its implementation. Clinton personally led negotiations at Camp David in July 2000.

The Bush Administration sought a less prominent role. In March 2001, Secretary of State Powell said that he would not appoint a special Middle East envoy to Arab-Israeli negotiations and that "the United States stands ready to assist, not insist. Only the parties themselves can determine the pace and scope and content of any negotiations ...." After the September 11, 2002 terrorist attacks on the United States, however, the Administration focused on the peace process because it needed to ensure Arab support for the war on terrorism. Nonetheless, the Administration still appears reluctant to become as deeply immersed in the peace process as its predecessor.

Conference Format and Developments

Madrid

On October 30, 1991, the conference opened. Parties were represented by 14-member delegations. A Jordanian/Palestinian delegation had 14 representatives from each. An unofficial Palestinian advisory team coordinated with the PLO. The United States, the Soviet Union, Syria, Palestinians/Jordan, the EC, Egypt, Israel, and Lebanon sat at the table. The U.N., the Gulf Cooperation Council, and the Arab Maghreb Union were observers.

Bilateral Talks

Israel-Palestinians

(Note: Because of space constraints, incidents of violence, terror, reprisals, and casualties are noted selectively.) On November 3, 1991, Israel and the

Jordanian/Palestinian delegation agreed to separate Israel-Jordan and Israel-Palestinians negotiating tracks, the latter to address a 5-year period of interim self-rule for Palestinians in the West Bank and Gaza Strip. In the third year, permanent status negotiations were to begin. On August 9, 1993, Palestinian negotiators were appointed to a PLO coordination committee, ending a charade that had distanced the PLO from the talks. Secret talks in Oslo since January 1993 produced an August 19 agreement on a Declaration of Principles, signed September 13, 1993. (For summaries of most accords, see **Agreements**, below.) Talks begun in October 1993 produced An Agreement on the Gaza Strip and the Jericho Area on May 4, 1994, which incorporated A Protocol on Economic Relations. It officially began the 5-year period of interim Palestinian self-rule. On September 28, 1995, Israel and the Palestinians signed an Interim Agreement. Israel began redeploying from the West Bank on October 10. Israeli Prime Minister Rabin was assassinated on November 4; Foreign Minister Peres succeeded him and redeployed from six cities, and from areas around Hebron by December. On January 20, 1996, Palestinians elected an 88-member Council and Yasir Arafat as Chairman. On April 24, the Palestine National Council (PNC) amended the Palestinian Charter by canceling "articles contrary to letters exchanged between the PLO and Israel in September 1993," i.e., those calling for the destruction of Israel. Final status talks on borders, security, settlements, refugees, water, and Jerusalem began ceremonially on May 5.

Binyamin Netanyahu was elected Prime Minister of Israel on May 29, 1996. His coalition's guidelines called for negotiations to reach a permanent arrangement only if the Palestinians fulfill all commitments fully, opposed the establishment of a Palestinian state west of the Jordan River, vowed to ensure the existence and security of Jewish settlements, and to keep Jerusalem under Israel's sovereignty. On August 2, his cabinet abolished most restraints on settlements. In September 1996, Palestinians protested violently against Israel's opening of an archaeological tunnel at the base of Jerusalem holy sites. After an October 1-2 summit, the two sides resumed talks and initialed a Protocol Concerning the Redeployment in Hebron on January 15, 1997. Israel redeployed from about 80% of Hebron.

On February 26, 1997, Israel approved construction of housing at Har Homa/Jabal Abu Ghneim in south East Jerusalem. On March 7, Israel's planned first of three further redeployments fell far short of the Palestinians' demands. On March 18, Israel broke ground at Har Homa. On July 30, a double suicide bombing in Jerusalem killed 13, including one American, and wounded 168. The President and Secretary of State called on the PA to make a 100% effort on security and sent Special Envoy Dennis Ross to the region. Israel and the PA agreed to report on the bombing to a panel including the CIA.

In September and October 1998, U.S. officials made a concerted effort to complete implementation of the Interim Accord, culminating in the Wye River Memorandum of October 23. The Israeli cabinet approved the Memorandum but said that redeployments depended on the abrogation of Palestinian Charter articles; that a third redeployment should not be from more than 1% of territory before a final agreement; and that if the Palestinians unilaterally declare a state, then Israel reserved the right to apply Israeli law to the rest of the West Bank.

On December 14, the PNC and others voted to annul the Charter articles. On December 20, Israel froze Wye implementation until the Palestinians abandoned their call for a state with Jerusalem as its capital, curbed violence and incitement, accepted Israeli prisoner releases, collected and destroyed illegal weapons, and resumed security cooperation. Europe and the United States forestalled a Palestinian declaration of statehood on May 4, 1999. In March, the European Union (EU) reaffirmed the "Palestinian right to self-determination including the option of a state ...." On April 26, President Clinton wrote, "We support the aspirations of the Palestinian people to determine their own future on their land."

Ehud Barak defeated Netanyahu in the May 17, 1999 election. Barak and Arafat signed the Sharm al-Shaykh Memorandum on September 4, 1999. Final status talks resumed ceremonially on September 13. The Palestinians gave Israel 30,000 police officers' names. Israel released prisoners, opened a safe passage between the West Bank and Gaza and a major road in Hebron, and redeployed from more territory. In May, Israeli soldiers fought Palestinian demonstrators and police.

Clinton, Barak, and Arafat held a summit at **Camp David**, from July 11 to July 24, to forge a framework accord on final status issues. They did not succeed. The parties had agreed that there would be no agreement unless all issues were resolved. Jerusalem was the major obstacle. Israel proposed that it remain united under its sovereignty, leaving the Palestinians control over East Jerusalem and Muslim holy sites. Israel was willing to cede more than 90% of the West Bank, wanted to annex settlements where about 130,000 settlers live, and offered to admit thousands of Palestinian refugees in a family unification program. An international fund would compensate other refugees as well as Israelis from Arab countries. The Palestinians reportedly were willing to accept Israeli control over the Jewish quarter of Jerusalem and the Western Wall but sought sovereignty over East Jerusalem, particularly the Haram al-Sharif/Temple Mount, a site holy to Jews and Muslims.

On September 28, Israeli opposition leader Ariel Sharon, with 1,000 security forces, visited the Temple Mount/Haram al-Sharif. Palestinians protested, and Israel responded forcefully. The second Palestinian *intifadah* or uprising began. On October 12, a mob in Ramallah killed two Israeli soldiers, provoking Israeli helicopter gunship attacks on Palestinian official sites. U.S. and other diplomats called a summit in Sharm al-Shaykh on October 16 and set up an international fact-finding committee to look into the violence.

Barak resigned on December 10, triggering an early election for Prime Minister. Further negotiations were held at Bolling Air Force Base, December 19-23. On December 23, President Clinton suggested that Israel cede sovereignty over the Temple Mount/Haram al-Sharif and Arab neighborhoods in Jerusalem and 96% of the West Bank and all of the Gaza Strip, and annex settlement blocs in exchange for giving the Palestinians Israeli land near Gaza. Jerusalem would be the capital of two countries. The Palestinians would cede the right of refugees to return to Israel and accept a Jewish "connection" to the Temple Mount and sovereignty over the Western Wall and holy sites beneath it. Israeli forces would remain in the Jordan Valley for 3 to 6 years to control borders, and then be replaced by an international force. The agreement would declare "an end to conflict." Barak said he would accept the plan as a basis for further talks if Arafat did so. Arafat sought clarifications on contiguity of Palestinian state territory, the division of East Jerusalem, and refugees' right of return, among other issues. The talks concluded at Taba, Egypt.

On February 6, 2001, Sharon was elected Prime Minister. He vowed to retain united Jerusalem as Israel's capital, the Jordan Valley and other security areas. Sharon's associates asserted that the results of negotiations at and since Camp David were "null and void." The Bush Administration said that Clinton's proposals "were no longer United States proposals." Sharon said that he sought an interim agreement, not dealing with Jerusalem, Palestinian refugees, or a Palestinian state. On April 13, Sharon said that he could accept a disarmed Palestinian state on 42% of the West Bank, about 2% more than the Palestinians control. Palestinians insisted that talks restart from where they left off at Taba.

On April 30, the international fact-finding commission led by former Senator George Mitchell submitted a report on the causes of the violence and made recommendations for ending it, rebuilding confidence, and resuming negotiations. On June 12, the two sides agreed to CIA Director Tenet's work plan to cement the cease-fire and restore security cooperation. On June 28, they agreed to a 7-day period without violence followed by a 6-week cooling-off period. Secretary Powell said Sharon would determine if violence abated.

On August 8, Hamas detonated a suicide bomb in Jerusalem. On August 10, Israeli forces seized Orient House, the center of Palestinian national activity in East Jerusalem, and then repeatedly entered Palestinian territory. On August 27, Israel killed the Popular Front for the Liberation of Palestine's (PFLP) leader. On September 24, Sharon declared, "Israel wants to give the Palestinians what no one else gave them before, the possibility of a state." On October 2, President Bush said for the first time, "The idea of a Palestinian state has always been part of a vision, so long as the right of Israel to exist is respected." Israel eased its blockade of Palestinian areas but stopped after the PFLP assassinated its Minister of Tourism on October 17.

On November 10, President Bush told the U.N. General Assembly that the United States is "working toward the day when two states – Israel and Palestine – live peacefully together within secure and recognized borders...." Secretary of State Powell sent retired General Anthony Zinni to work on a durable cease-fire to revive peacemaking, but violence escalated before and surged after Zinni arrived on November 26. Israel confined Arafat in Ramallah on December 3. On December 7, Sharon said that "it's hard to believe that one can get into an agreement with Arafat, who is a real terrorist...." On December 12, Hamas ambushed an Israeli bus in the West Bank and perpetrated two simultaneous suicide bombings in Gaza. The Israeli security cabinet charged that Arafat was "directly responsible" for the attacks ... "and therefore is no longer relevant ...." On December 16, Zinni was recalled; Arafat called for "a comprehensive cessation of all armed activities ... especially suicide attacks."

On January 3, 2002, Israel seized a Palestinian-commanded freighter, the Karine A, in the Red Sea carrying 50 tons of Iranian-supplied arms. On February 5, Secretary Powell stated that Arafat "cannot engage with us and others in the pursuit of peace, and at the same time permit or tolerate continued violence and terror." When Sharon visited the White House on February 7, he said that he believed that pressure should be put on Arafat so that an alternative Palestinian leadership could emerge.

On February 28, Israeli ground forces launched an assault on West Bank refugee camps, "bases of terror infrastructure," beginning a three-week reoccupation of Palestinian areas. Suicide bombers and gunmen from Al Aqsa, the PIJ, Hamas, and the PFLP continued to exact a high toll on Israelis. President Bush sent General Zinni back to the region. On March 14, President Bush said that Israel's reoccupation was "not helpful." Israel withdrew by March 19. After March 20, there were daily suicide bombings.

On February 17, Saudi Crown Prince Abdullah had called for "full withdrawal from all occupied territories, in accord with U.N. resolutions, including Jerusalem, for full normalization of relations." Sharon said that he was willing to explore the idea but it would be a "mistake" to replace U.N. resolutions affirming Israel's right to "secure and recognized borders" with total withdrawal to pre-1967 borders. On March 27, the Arab League summit Beirut Declaration endorsed Abdullah's offer of "normal relations and security for Israel in exchange for full withdrawal from the occupied Arab territories, recognition of an independent Palestinian state with al-Quds al Sharif (Noble Jerusalem) as its capital, and the return of refugees." The summit communique saluted the Palestinian *intifadah* and called for stopping the establishment of ties with Israel.

Also on March 27, a Hamas suicide bomber attacked an Israeli hotel in Netanya, killing 27 and wounding 130. The Israeli cabinet declared Arafat "an enemy" and, on March 29, sent troops to besiege his compound in Ramallah, beginning war on the "terrorist infrastructure." Within a week, Israeli forces controlled all major Palestinian-ruled West Bank cities. U.N. Security Council Resolution 1402, March 30, called on the parties to move immediately to a meaningful cease-fire and on Israel to withdraw.

On April 4, President Bush chastised Arafat, Arab nations, and Israel, and urged Israel to begin withdrawing from Palestinian areas. On April 6, he emphasized that Israel must withdraw "without delay." Secretary Powell met moderate Arab, U.N., and EU leaders and representatives before arriving in Israel on April 10. During his visit, there were suicide bombings in Haifa and Jerusalem. On April 14, Sharon proposed that the United States host a regional conference without Arafat. On April 15, Powell said that a ministerial-level conference might lead to a political track quickly. On May 2, the Quartet, i.e., U.S., EU, U.N., and Russian officials, proposed a foreign ministers' conference to discuss reconstructing the PA and economic and humanitarian issues. At Sharon's May 8 visit, the President emphasized providing "the framework for the growth of a Palestinian state," while Sharon said that it is premature to discuss a state until he sees "real reform." During the meeting, a Hamas suicide bombing occurred south of Tel Aviv.

On May 14, Sharon again called for "the complete cessation of terror, violence, and incitement, and basic structural reforms in all areas of the Palestinian Authority" before negotiations for a settlement in stages. On May 15, Arafat called for "speedy preparations" for elections and for the restructuring of the PA. Assistant Secretary of State for Near East Affairs Burns and CIA Director Tenet traveled to the region as part of what President Bush termed a strategy to combine security and democratization as underpinnings of a Palestinian state. After meeting Sharon on June 9, President Bush said that conditions were not ripe for a ministerial meeting because "no one has confidence" in the Palestinian government.

On June 24, President Bush called on the Palestinians to elect new leaders "not compromised by terror" and to build a practicing democracy. (See White House press release [http://www.whitehouse.gov/news/releases/2002/06/20020624-3.html].) He said that when the Palestinians have new leaders, new institutions, and new security arrangements with their neighbors, then the United States will support the creation of a Palestinian state, whose borders and certain aspects of sovereignty will be provisional until a final settlement. He added, "as we make progress toward security, Israeli forces need to withdraw fully to positions they held prior to September 28, 2000 ... and settlement activity must stop." The President envisaged a final settlement within 3 years negotiated by the parties "based on U.N. Resolutions 242 and 338, with Israeli withdrawal to secure and recognized borders."

On July 16, the Quartet set an International Task Force on Reform to "develop and implement a comprehensive action plan for reform." On July 31, Hamas set off a bomb at the Hebrew University in Jerusalem, killing 7, including 5 Americans, and wounding 80.

On August 18, the Israeli Defense Minister and the Palestinian Interior Minister agreed that Israel would cede responsibility for the security of Bethlehem and parts of Gaza to the Palestinian police. If the police succeeded in preventing terrorism, then Israeli forces would withdraw from other areas. On August 19, Israeli troops withdrew from Bethlehem but kept a blockade around it. The process then stalled. Hamas, Palestine Islamic Jihad (PIJ), and Damascus-based Palestinian groups denounced the accord and vowed to continue attacks.

On September 17, the Quartet outlined a "road map" to peace: the first phase would see Palestinian security reform, Israeli withdrawals, and support for Palestinian elections to be held in early 2003. The second phase, in 2003, would create a Palestinian state with provisional borders and a new constitution. Finally, Israeli-Palestinian negotiations in 2004 to mid-2005 would lead to a permanent settlement and Palestinian statehood. (The road map has not been published officially. See [http://www.washingtoninstitute.org] for two reported drafts.)

More than six weeks of relative quiet ended with two suicide bombings in 24 hours on September 19. On September 20-21, Israeli forces demolished buildings at Arafat's headquarters in Ramallah and demanded the surrender of "wanted men" in the compound. On September 24, the United States abstained from U.N. Security Council Resolution1435, which demanded an immediate end to Israel's reoccupation of Arafat's headquarters and expeditious withdrawal from

Palestinian cities; it also condemned terror attacks against civilians. Israel lifted its siege of Arafat's compound on September 29.

On October 7, Israeli forces raided Khan Yunis in the southern Gaza Strip. The Administration was "deeply concerned" about civilian casualties. Israeli forces withdrew from parts of the West Bank and eased restrictions in others. On October 17, Israeli forces battled Palestinian gunmen in a Gaza refugee camp. On October 21, the PIJ perpetrated a suicide car bombing in northern Israel. Israeli forces reoccupied Jenin and swept into other cities. On November 10, a gunman infiltrated a kibbutz in northern Israel and killed 5. On November 15, PIJ gunmen ambushed Israeli security forces in Hebron, killing 12 and wounding about 30. On November 21, a Hamas suicide bomber blew up a bus in Jerusalem. Israel declared the August "Bethlehem first" agreement "null and void" and Israeli forces reoccupied the city. On November 29, the Al Aqsa Martyrs' Brigade claimed an attack on a Likud polling station in Beit She'an in Israel. Israel made more incursions into West Bank cities and Gaza Strip refugee camps and killed alleged terrorist leaders.

On December 18, Secretary Powell said that it would be wiser to wait until after the January 28 Israeli election to make the road map public. A revised road map reportedly called on the Palestinians to take unconditional steps to halt violence and conditions the establishment of a Palestinian state on the leaders' moves against terrorism and the establishment of democracy. President Bush met with the Quartet on December 21. A joint statement condemned Palestinian terror attacks and the killing of innocent Palestinian civilians. It called for an immediate cease-fire and "as calm is established, Israeli forces should withdraw from Palestinian areas and the pre-intifadah status quo on the ground should be restored." It also called for reform of Palestinian security services and on Israel to ease the humanitarian situation in the West Bank and Gaza Strip.

On January 5, 2003, two Palestinian bombers blew themselves up in Tel Aviv, killing 23 and wounding 100. Israel imposed a travel ban on the West Bank and Gaza Strip, refused to allow most Palestinian Central Committee members attend a meeting to ratify a new constitution, banned Palestinians younger than 35 from entering Israel, and said that it would close three Palestinian universities (it closed two). Israel barred Palestinians from attending a conference on reform with the Quartet, Egyptian, Saudi, and Jordanian officials on January 14-15 at the invitation of British Prime Minister Blair. The Palestinians submitted an outline for a constitution to establish a government of separation of powers, a prime minister, and independent judiciary. The British host said that there was recognition that without credible Palestinian performance on security, reforms would founder.

On January 20, Sharon told an interviewer, "the Quartet is nothing! Don't take it seriously." Secretary Powell responded that Washington remained "fully supportive of the quartet, which we helped create." On January 26, Israeli forces made their deepest incursion into Gaza City in 2 years to target weapons factories, killing 12 and injuring more than 40. A landmine destroyed an Israeli tank and killed its crew on February 15; the Israeli military then began persistent operations in the Gaza Strip, targeting Hamas. After Palestinians fired rockets into southern Israel, Israeli forces blocked two main roads in the Gaza Strip. They continued to make incursions into West Bank cities. On March 5, a suicide bomber destroyed a bus in Haifa, killing 16, including one American, and wounding about 55. Israeli forces then raided a Gaza refugee camp, killing 11, and reoccupied an area of northern Gaza. The Palestinians say that civilians were more than half of the victims in Gaza in February and March.

On February 24, Sharon formed a coalition government with the National Religious Party, an advocate for settlers and opponent of a Palestinian state, and Shinui, as secular party that favors, with changes, the road map, but without Arafat and the refugees' right of return. Sharon then brought in the National Union; some of whose members favor expelling Palestinians from and annexing the territories. The government's guidelines call for reaching interim agreements with the Palestinians when violence ends and declare that settlement is an important national project. Negotiations on statehood require cabinet approval.

On February 27, President Bush said that, as the terror threat is removed and security improves, Israel will be expected to support the creation of a viable Palestinian state and to work quickly toward a final status agreement. "As progress is made toward peace," settlement activity must end. The President gave his personal commitment to implement the road map.

On March 7, Arafat named Mahmud Abbas (aka Abu Mazen) Prime Minister, but Arafat kept control over security forces and foreign (peace) policy. The United States, Israel, and the U.N. called for empowering the prime minister to work on peace. Secretary of State Powell said that Abbas's appointment "is a positive step forward."

Israel-Syria

Syria seeks to regain sovereignty over the Golan Heights, 450 square miles of land along the border that Israel seized in 1967. Israel applied its law and administration to the region in December 1981, an act other governments do not recognize. Syria initially referred to its goal as an end to the state of belligerency, not a peace treaty, preferred a comprehensive Arab-Israeli peace, and disdained separate agreements between Israel and Arab parties. Israel emphasized peace, defined as open borders, diplomatic, cultural, and commercial relations, security, and access to water resources.

In 1992, Israel agreed that 242 applies to all fronts. Syria submitted a draft declaration of principles, reportedly referring to a "peace agreement." Israeli Prime Minister Rabin accepted withdrawal on the Golan, without defining it, pending Syria's definition of "peace." On September 23, 1992, the Syrian Foreign Minister promised "total peace in exchange for total withdrawal." Israel offered only "withdrawal." In 1993, Syrian President Asad announced interest in peace and suggested that bilateral tracks might progress at different speeds. In June, Secretary Christopher said that the United States might be willing to guarantee security arrangements in the context of a sound agreement on the Golan.

On January 16, 1994, President Clinton reported that Asad had told him that Syria was ready for talks about "normal peaceful relations" with Israel. The sides inched toward each other on a withdrawal and normalization timetable. Asad again told President Clinton on October 27 that he was committed to normal peaceful relations in return for full withdrawal. Israeli and Syrian chiefs of staff met in December.

On March 20, 1995, ambassadorial talks resumed. On May 24, Israel and Syria announced terms of reference for senior military experts to meet under U.S. auspices. Syria reportedly conceded that demilitarized and thinned-out zones may take topographical features into account and be unequal, if security arrangements were equal. Chiefs of staff discussed principles for security arrangements. Israel offered Syria an early-warning ground station in northern Israel in exchange for Golan stations, but Syria insisted on aerial surveillance only and that each country monitor the other from its own territory and receive U.S. satellite photographs. It was proposed that Syria demilitarize 6 miles for every 3.6 miles Israel demilitarizes. Rabin said that Israeli troops must man early-warning stations on the Golan after its return to Syria. Syria said that this would infringe on its sovereignty, but a government-controlled media commentary accepted international or friendly forces in the stations. Talks resumed at the Wye Plantation in Maryland in December 1995, but were suspended when Israeli negotiators went home after terrorist attacks in February/March 1996.

The new Israeli government called for negotiations, but said that the Golan is essential to Israel's security and water needs and that retaining sovereignty would be the basis for an arrangement with Syria. Asad would not agree to talks unless Israel honored prior understandings, claiming that Rabin had promised total withdrawal to the June 4, 1967 border (as opposed to the international border of 1923). Israeli negotiators contend that Rabin had suggested full withdrawal was possible only if Syria met Israel's security and normalization needs and those needs were not met. On January 26, 1999, the Israeli Knesset passed a law requiring a 61-member majority and a national referendum to approve the return of any part of the Golan Heights to Syria.

In June, Prime Minister-elect Barak and Asad exchanged compliments through a British writer. In July, Syrian Vice President Khaddam told radical Palestinian groups to end their armed struggle against Israel and Syria prevented Hizballah from firing rockets into Israel, but not from targeting Israeli forces in south Lebanon. Israel and Syria agreed to restart talks from "the point where they left off," with each side defining the point to its satisfaction. Barak and Syrian Foreign Minister led delegations to Washington on December 15-16, 1999, and to Shepherdstown, WV, from January 3-10, 2000. President Clinton intervened. On January 7, the United States presented a summary of points of accord and discord. As published by an Israeli newspaper, it revealed Israel's apparent success in delaying discussion of borders and winning concessions on normal relations and an early-warning station. Reportedly because of Syrian anger over the leak of the document, talks scheduled to resume on January 19, 2000, were "postponed indefinitely."

On March 26, President Clinton met Asad in Geneva. A White House spokesman reported "significant differences remain" and said that it would not be productive for talks to resume. Barak indicated that disagreements centered on Israel's reluctance to withdraw to the June 1967 border and cede access to the Sea of Galilee, on security arrangements, and on the early-warning station. Syria agreed that the border/Sea issue had been the main obstacle. Asad died on June 10; his son, Bashar, succeeded him. Ariel Sharon became Prime Minister of Israel in February 2001 and vowed to retain the Golan Heights.

Israel-Lebanon

As called for by Security Council Resolution 425, Lebanon sought unconditional Israeli military withdrawal from the 9-mile "security zone" in southern Lebanon and the end of Israel's support for militias in the south and of shelling of villages that Israel claimed were sites of Hizballah activity. Israel claimed no Lebanese territory but sought security and said that it would withdraw when the Lebanese army controlled the south and prevented Hizballah attacks on northern Israel. Lebanon repeatedly sought a withdrawal schedule in exchange for addressing Israel's security concerns. The two sides never agreed. Syria, which dominates Lebanon, said that Israel-Syria progress should come first. In July 1993, Israel conducted a large assault to stop Hizballah attacks; 250,000 people fled south Lebanon. Secretary of State Christopher arranged a cease-fire. In March/April 1996, Israel again attacked Hizballah targets, and Hizballah fired rockets into northern Israel. An April 26 cease-fire accord barred Hizballah attacks into Israel and Israeli attacks on civilian targets in Lebanon and all attacks on civilians or civilian areas. Each side retained the right of self-defense. U.S., French, Syrian, Lebanese, and Israeli representatives monitored the cease-fire.

On January 5, 1998, Defense Minister Mordechai said that Israel was ready to withdraw from southern Lebanon if the second part of Resolution 425, calling for the restoration of peace and security in the region, were implemented. He and Netanyahu then proposed that Israel withdraw in exchange for security, not peace and normalization. Lebanon and Syria called for an unconditional Israeli withdrawal. Violence in northern Israel and southern Lebanon increased in November and December, prompting the Israeli cabinet to reaffirm its opposition to a unilateral withdrawal twice. In April 1999, Israel "downsized" its force in Lebanon. In June, the Israeli-allied South Lebanese Army (SLA) withdrew from Jazzin, north of the security zone. New Prime Minister Barak promised to withdraw from southern Lebanon in one year, or by July 7, 2000, while maintaining security for northern Israel.

On September 4, 1999, Lebanese Prime Minister Al-Hoss confirmed his country's commitment to 425 and support for the "resistance" against the occupation, i.e., Hizballah. He argued that Palestinian refugees residing in Lebanon have the right to return to their homeland, and rejected their implantation in Lebanon. Al-Hoss did not accept Secretary of State Albright's statement that Palestinian refugees in Lebanon will be a subject of Israeli-Palestinian final status talks, insisting that Lebanon should be a party to such talks.

On March 5, 2000, the Israeli cabinet voted to withdraw from southern Lebanon by July. Lebanon warned that it would not guarantee security for northern Israel unless Israel also withdrew from the Golan and worked to resolve the refugee issue. On April 17, Israel informed the U.N. of its plan. On May 12, Lebanon informed the U.N. that Israel's withdrawal would not be complete unless it included Sheba'a farms near the Golan. On May 23, the U.N. Secretary General noted that almost all of Sheba'a is within the area of operations of the U.N. Disengagement Observer Force (UNDOF) overseeing the 1974 Israeli-Syrian disengagement, and recommended proceeding without prejudice to later border agreements. On May 23, the SLA collapsed, and on May 24 Israel completed its withdrawal. Hizballah took over the former security zone. On June 18, the U.N. Security Council agreed that Israel had withdrawn. The U.N. Interim Force in Lebanon (UNIFIL) deployed only 400 troops to the border region by July, because the Lebanese army did not back them against Hizballah.

On October 7, Hizballah shelled northern Israel and captured three Israeli soldiers. (Israel has since declared them to be dead.) On October 16, Hizballah announced that it had captured an Israeli colonel. On November 13, U.N. Security Council members said that Lebanon was obliged to "take effective control of the whole area vacated by Israel ...." On April 16 and July 2, 2001, Israel, claiming Syria controls Hizballah, bombed Syrian radar sites in Lebanon after Hizballah attacked its soldiers in Sheba'a. In April, the U.N. warned Lebanon that unless it deployed to the border, UNIFIL would be diminished or phased out. On January 28, 2002, the Security Council voted to cut UNIFIL to 2,000 by the end of 2002.

During Israel's military operations against Palestinian-ruled areas, on March 29 and subsequently, Hizballah shelled Israeli positions in Sheba'a and northern Israel. Israel responded with air strikes, and concern about a possible second front. At its request, U.N. Secretary General Annan contacted the Syrian and Lebanese Presidents, and on April 8, Vice President Cheney called President Asad to warn him that the situation could spiral out of control. Syria denied that it or Lebanon is interested in opening a second front. In April, Secretary Powell visited Israel's northern command and called on Syria to curb Hizballah, and while in Lebanon and Syria urged them to stop the attacks immediately. The shelling stopped briefly and then resumed. There is a dispute over Lebanon's plan to pump water from the Wazzani River, which Israel said would reduce the flow of water into the Galilee.

Israel-Jordan

Of Jordan's 3.4 million people, 55 to 70% are Palestinian; government figures acknowledge 40%. An estimated 300,000 Palestinians displaced by the Gulf War fled to Jordan. Jordan hoped an Israel-Palestinian accord would ease its economic problems by producing international aid. Jordan would not ratify a June 1993 agenda on water, energy, environment, and economic matters before other Arab parties reached accords. It was initialed on September 14, 1993, after the Israeli-Palestinian DOP was signed.

Rabin reportedly met King Hussein secretly on September 26, 1993. On October 1, Crown Prince Hassan, Foreign Minister Peres, and President Clinton agreed to set up a Trilateral Economic Committee. In June 1994, Israel and Jordan held talks on boundaries, water, energy, moving talks to the region, and trade and economic relations. Rabin and King Hussein opened a border crossing for third country tourists on August 8. A peace treaty was signed on October 26 (see **Agreements** below). The border was demarcated and Israel withdrew from Jordanian land on February 9, 1995. More agreements followed.

On March 9, 1997, King Hussein charged that Netanyahu was "bent on destroying the peace process...." On September 25, 1997, Israeli agents failed to assassinate a Hamas official in Jordan. King Hussein demanded that Israel release Hamas founder Shaykh Yasmin, which it did on October 1, with 70 Jordanian and

Palestinian prisoners in exchange for the detained agents. On December 5, 1998, the King again lambasted Netanyahu. He called for Jordan-Palestinian coordination, observing that many final status issues are Jordanian national interests. King Hussein died on February 7, 1999.

On February 28, 1999, Netanyahu and King Abdullah II reaffirmed their dedication to peace. Abdullah has said that the Palestinians should administer the Muslim holy sites in Jerusalem, a traditional responsibility of the Jordanian royal family, but rejected a Jordanian-Palestinian confederation. He said that warmer relations with Israel depend upon progress toward peace with the Palestinians and Syria, and proposed that Jerusalem be an Israeli and a Palestinian capital. On November 21, 2000, Jordan stopped accreditation of its new ambassador to Israel because of Israel's "aggression" against the Palestinians.

Significant Agreements

Israel-PLO Mutual Recognition

On September 9, 1993, Arafat recognized Israel's right to exist, accepted U.N. Security Council Resolutions 242 and 338, the Middle East peace process, and the peaceful resolution of conflicts. He renounced terrorism and violence and undertook to prevent them, stated that articles of the Palestinian Charter that contradict his commitments are invalid, undertook to submit Charter changes to the Palestine National Council, and called upon his people to reject violence. Rabin recognized the PLO as the representative of the Palestinian people and agreed to negotiate with it.

Declaration of Principles

On August 29, 1993, Israel and the Palestinians announced that they had agreed on a Declaration of Principles on interim self-government for the West Bank and Gaza on August 19, after secret negotiations in Oslo, Norway, since January 1993. Effective October 13, it called for Palestinian self-rule in Gaza and Jericho; transfer of authority over education, culture, health, social welfare, direct taxation, and tourism in the West Bank and Gaza to Palestinians; election in 9 months of a Palestinian Council with jurisdiction over the West Bank and Gaza; Palestinian residents of East Jerusalem will vote; Israeli troops to redeploy from Palestinian population centers before the election and further as Palestinian police assume responsibility for public order; joint Israeli-Palestinian committees for issues such as economic cooperation and dispute resolution; the parties to invite

Jordan and Egypt to establish cooperative arrangements that will decide modalities of admission of persons displaced in 1967, etc. During the interim period, Israel responsible for external security, settlements, Israelis, and foreign relations. Permanent status negotiations will begin in the third year of interim rule and may include Jerusalem.

Israel-Jordan Agenda

Initialed on September 14, 1993, with sections on security, water, refugees and displaced persons, borders and territorial matters, bilateral cooperation on natural and human resources, infrastructure, and economic areas. Reaffirms the 1967 international border; Israel to withdraw from two small strips of land seized in 1968.

Agreement on the Gaza Strip and the Jericho Area

Signed on May 4, 1994, provides for Israeli withdrawal from Gaza/Jericho to begin immediately and to be complete within three weeks. Israel to evacuate all military bases, hand them over to Palestinian police, and redeploy to settlements and military installations. Israelis may use roads within Gaza/Jericho and Palestinians may use public roads crossing settlements. Palestinian police to be responsible for public order and internal security. Authority to be transferred from the Israeli military government and civil administration to the PA. The PA will consist of 24 members with legislative and executive powers and established administrative units. The Authority's territorial jurisdiction includes land, subsoil, and territorial waters. Israel retains jurisdiction over foreign relations, external security, and security of settlements. The PLO may conclude economic, assistance, and regional development agreements with international organizations and foreign states. The PA may promulgate laws, regulations, and other legislative acts. The Palestinians may have a police force, but not other armed forces. Israel is to release 5,000 Palestinian prisoners within five weeks and negotiate release of others. The parties agree to a Temporary International Presence of 400 for 6 months. The accord began the 5-year period of interim self-rule.

The Washington Declaration

Signed on July 25, 1994. Terminates state of belligerency; King Hussein declared an end to the state of war at the signing ceremony.

Israel-Jordan Peace Treaty

Signed on October 26, 1994. An international boundary will be delimited within 9 months with reference to that of the former British Mandate. Each party will refrain from threats or use of force against the other and from joining alliances hostile to the other and will remove restrictions from normal economic relations and terminate economic boycotts. Problems of displaced persons (from 1967) will be resolved in a committee with Egypt and the Palestinians and of refugees (from 1948) in the multilateral framework. Israel respects Jordan's role in the mosques in Jerusalem and will give it high priority in permanent status negotiations. Unrevealed annexes reportedly called for Jordan to lease one sq. mi. to Israelis for a renewable 25-year period and for Israel to provide Yarmuk River water and desalinized water to Jordan; dams will be built on the Yarmuk and Jordan Rivers to yield more water.

Israeli-Palestinian Interim Agreement, West Bank — Gaza Strip

(Also called the Taba Accords or Oslo II.) Signed on September 28, 1995. Annexes deal with security arrangements, elections, civil affairs, legal matters, economic relations, Israeli-Palestinian cooperation, and the release of Palestinian prisoners. Negotiations on permanent status and relations with neighboring countries will begin in May 1996. An 82-member Palestinian Council and Head of the Council's Executive Authority will be elected after Israeli redeployment from populated areas in the West Bank. Palestinian residents of Jerusalem will participate in the elections by mail and may stand for election if they have a second address in the West Bank or Gaza. The Israeli Defense Force will redeploy from Jenin, Nablus, Tulkarm, Qalqilyah, Ramallah, and Bethlehem, and 450 towns and villages. Israel will redeploy in Hebron, except where necessary for security of Israelis. Israel will be responsible for external security and the security of Israelis and settlements. Palestinians will be totally responsible for Area "A," the six cities. Israeli responsibility for overall security will have precedence over Palestinian responsibility for public order in Area "B," Palestinian towns and villages. Israel will retain full responsibility in Area "C," unpopulated areas.

Further redeployments will take place in 6-month intervals following the Council's inauguration, with Palestinians gaining territorial jurisdiction over more of Area C, subject to land rights of Israelis and provision of services to settlements. Palestinian Charter articles calling for the destruction of Israel will be revoked within two months of the Council's inauguration. Israel and the Palestinians will cooperate against terrorism. Palestinians will have a police force of 12,000, issue arms' permits, and confiscate illegal arms. Israelis may not be arrested by Palestinian police. Responsibility for religious sites will be transferred to the Palestinians, with freedom of access and of worship guaranteed. Israel will increase water allocated to Palestinians. Further increases to be based on increases in resources developed though international funding and channels, including the

U.S.-Palestinian-Israeli forum. Israel will release Palestinian prisoners in three stages: upon signing of the agreement, on the eve of elections, and according to other principles to be established. Economic Annex of the Gaza-Jericho Agreement, with minor changes, is incorporated.

Protocol Concerning the Redeployment in Hebron

Initialed by Israel and the PA on January 15, 1997. Details security arrangements. In Notes for the Record, Israel agreed to prisoner release and to resume negotiations on safe passage between Gaza and the West Bank, Gaza Airport and port, economic, and other issues. The Palestinians reaffirmed their commitment to revise their Charter, to fight terror, and to keep police force size in line with the Interim accord. Permanent status negotiations were to resume within two months after implementation of the Protocol. Christopher wrote a letter to Netanyahu, stating that it remains U.S. policy to promote full implementation of the Interim Agreement and that he had advised Arafat that Israeli redeployments would be completed no later than mid-1998–defined by U.S. Special Envoy Ross as August 1998.

Wye River Memorandum

Signed on October 23, 1998. Delineates steps to be taken over a 12-week period to complete implementation of the Interim Agreement and of agreements specified in Notes for the Record that accompanied the Hebron Protocol. Israel will redeploy from territories in the West Bank in exchange for Palestinian security measures. The PA will have complete or shared responsibility for 40% of the West Bank, of which it will have complete control of 18.2%. Palestinians ensure systematic combat of terrorist organizations and their infrastructure. Their work plan will be shared with the United States. A U.S.-Palestinian committee will review steps to counter terrorism. The Palestinians will prohibit illegal weapons. The Palestinians will prohibit incitement to violence and terror and establish mechanisms to act against provocateurs.

A U.S.-Palestinian-Israeli committee will monitor incitement and recommend how to prevent it. Israeli-Palestinian security cooperation will be full, continuous, and comprehensive. A trilateral committee will meet not less than biweekly to assess threats and deal with impediments to cooperation. The Palestinians will provide a list of their policemen to the Israelis. The PLO Executive and Central Committees will reaffirm the January 22, 1998, letter from Arafat to President Clinton that specified articles of the Palestinian Charter that had been nullified in April 1996. The Palestine National Council will reaffirm these decisions. President Clinton will address this conclave. The two sides agreed on a Gaza industrial estate and on a protocol for opening the Gaza airport. They agreed to work to agree on safe passage between the Gaza Strip and West Bank and on a Gaza seaport. Permanent status talks will resume when the Memorandum takes effect. A time line is an "integral attachment" to the Memorandum. U.S. officials provided both sides with letters of assurance regarding U.S. policies.

Sharm al-Shaykh Memorandum

(Also called Wye II.) Signed on September 4, 1999. Agreed to resume permanent status negotiations in an accelerated manner by September 13, to make a determined effort to conclude a framework agreement on permanent status issues in five months, and to conclude a comprehensive agreement on permanent status within one year or by September 13, 2000. They also agreed on other Wye issues.

Role of Congress

Aid

The Middle East Peace Facilitation Act (MEPFA) (P.L. 103-236, April 30, 1994, Title X) granted the President authority to suspend provisions of laws affecting the PLO in the national interest and if the PLO is abiding by commitments made in letters to Israel and Norway and under the DOP. The State Department reported that the PLO honored its commitments, with shortcomings, and asserted that suspensions were in the U.S. national interest, enabling U.S. support for the peace process and interaction with all parties. MEPFA was extended with additional requirements, until August 12, 1997, and then included in foreign operations appropriations legislation. P.L. 107-115, January 10, 2002 prohibits funds for the PA unless the President certifies that it is important to U.S. national security interests. P.L. 107-206, August, 2, 2002, a supplemental appropriation for FY2002 provided $200 million in aid to Israel to combat terrorism and $50 million in humanitarian aid to the Palestinians, not to the PA. P.L. 107-228, September 30, 2002, withheld $10 million in economic aid to Lebanon until its armed forces deploy to and assert the government's authority in south Lebanon. P.L. 108-1, February 20, 2003, prohibits funding to support a Palestinian state unless it has leaders who have not supported terrorism, have been democratically elected, have demonstrated their commitment to peaceful coexistence with Israel, have taken measures to counter terrorism and terrorism financing, and have established security entities that cooperate with Israeli counterparts. An exemption is provided for assistance to reform the PA and waiver is provided to the President for national security interests. Funding for the PA is prohibited. H.R. 1559 and S. 762, wartime supplemental appropriations bills passed on April 2, 2003, appropriate $9 billion in loan guarantees to Israel, but funds may be used only within its pre-June 5, 1967, borders.

Jerusalem

Jerusalem is a subject for final status negotiations. Israel annexed the city in 1967 to be its eternal, undivided capital. Palestinians seek East Jerusalem as their capital. Successive U.S. Administrations have maintained that the parties must determine its fate. H.Con.Res. 60, June 10, 1997, and S.Con.Res. 21, May 20, 1997, called on the Administration to affirm that Jerusalem must remain the undivided capital of Israel. Congress prohibits official U.S. government business with the PA in Jerusalem and the use of appropriated funds to create U.S. government offices in Israel to conduct business with the PA. (See P.L. 108-7, February 20, 2003.) H.R. 167, introduced on January 7, 2003, calls for the U.S. consulate in Jerusalem to operate under the supervision of the ambassador, for Jerusalem to be identified as the capital of Israel in official documents, and for Israel to be recorded as the place of birth of U.S. citizens born in Jerusalem.

A related issue is the relocation of the U.S. Embassy from Tel Aviv to Jerusalem. Proponents argue that Israel is the only country where a U.S. embassy is not in the capital, that Israel's claim to West Jerusalem, proposed site of an embassy, is unquestioned, and that Palestinians must be disabused of their hope for a capital in Jerusalem. Opponents say a move would undermine the peace process, U.S. credibility in the Islamic world and with Palestinians, and prejudge final status. P.L. 104-45, November 8, 1995, provided for the relocation of the embassy by May 31, 1999, but granted the President authority, in national security interest, to suspend limitations on State Department expenditures that would be imposed if the embassy did not open. Presidents Clinton and Bush each used the authority. The President signed H.R. 1646, the State Department Authorization Act for FY2002-2003, into law as P.L. 107-228, September 30, 2002. It urges the President to begin relocating the U.S. Embassy "immediately," and contains the same provisions as H.R. 167 noted above. The President charged that the provision would "if construed as mandatory rather than advisory, impermissibly interfere with the president's constitutional authority to conduct the nation's foreign affairs." The State Department declared, "our view of Jerusalem is unchanged. Jerusalem is a permanent status issue to be negotiated between the parties."

Compliance/Sanctions

S.Con.Res. 88 and H.Con.Res. 280, both passed on December 5, 2001, demand that the PA act against terrorists and urge the President to suspend relations with Arafat and the PA if it does not. P.L. 107-115, January 10, 2002, Sec. 566 left it to the President to assess PLO/PA compliance with its 1993 commitments and, if there is none, to impose sanctions. A November 9, 2002 State Department report, mandated by the PLO Commitments Compliance Act (P.L. 101-246), noted the PLO and PA failed to act against, and in some cases provided support for, terrorist groups as well as citing other noncompliance. It imposed the sanction of downgrading the status of the PLO office in the United States but waived the sanction in the interest of national security.

Chapter 7

MIDDLE EAST: ATTITUDES TOWARD THE UNITED STATES

Alfred B. Prados

INTRODUCTION

Despite close cooperation between the United States and some Middle Eastern states, serious tensions have often marred U.S. relations with Arabs and other Muslims in the Middle East. Popular sentiment in the Middle East, sometimes referred to as the "Arab street," has become increasingly important in its ability to influence regional policies as it has benefitted from the expansion in reach, availability, and sophistication of media outlets. Although there is much ambivalence on the "Arab street" regarding the United States, popular attitudes among Arabs and other Muslims in this region appear unfavorable toward the United States on various issues, which are summarized below.

As the lone remaining superpower, the United States has become a convenient target for discontent among much of the world's population. In the Middle East in particular, there is a tendency to blame U.S.-led globalization for the region's economic ills, despite the failure of Middle Eastern regimes themselves to adopt policies that would contribute toward greater economic growth.

There is a widespread perception in the region of U.S. society as fundamentally alien, if not hostile, to Islamic beliefs and values. At the same time, many Middle Easterners are attracted to the democratic principles and economic opportunities they find in the United States.

The deployment of U.S. armed forces contingents in the Middle East, particularly Saudi Arabia (where Islam's holiest cites are located), offends many in the region. These forces, however, maintain a generally low profile.

Many in the region blame U.S. containment policies for the continued sufferings of the Iraqi people. U.S. officials counter that Iraqi polices have caused the country's economic privations and warn that it would be risky to abandon containment measures until Iraq honors pertinent U.N. resolutions.

A common perception that U.S. policy is biased toward Israel has been a frequently cited cause of Arab and Muslim resentment. U.S. administrations, however, have devoted major efforts to solve the Arab-Israeli conflict.

Among the "Arab street" there is some resentment over the U.S. role in bolstering regimes that are perceived as oppressive, corrupt, or un-Islamic. These governments play important roles, however, in U.S. policy, and several have instituted reforms.

Various measures have been suggested to improve Middle East perceptions of the United States: expanded aid and trade enhancement programs; efforts to counter unfavorable images; attempts to secure wider backing for containing Iraq, while fine-tuning economic sanctions; agreement on a new framework for Arab-Israeli negotiations; encouragement of more open political systems in the Middle East. Local resentments, however, will not vanish overnight.

OVERVIEW

The United States has enjoyed close relations with Arab and Muslim states in the Middle East since the region emerged in its present configuration after the two world wars. U.S. economic and military assistance has played a major role in the development of important regional states such as Egypt and Jordan. Oil rich countries in the Persian Gulf region have been essential suppliers of energy resources to the United States and its industrial allies and major purchasers of U.S. commercial and military equipment. These ties have helped create a network of organizational relationships, official and personal contacts, bilateral economic and military commissions, and joint commercial endeavors between the United States and friendly countries in the Middle East.

Despite this extensive cooperation, serious tensions have often marred U.S. relations with Arabs and Muslims in the Middle East, both at governmental and popular levels. Some governments and sub-national groups in the region are avowedly hostile to the United States, oppose its policies on a broad spectrum of issues, and seek to damage U.S. interests in the region, sometimes through violence. This is particularly true of those governments that the U.S. State Department identified as supporters of international terrorism, as well as a number of militia-type groups that the State Department lists as foreign terrorist organizations. Even friendly governments in the Middle East are ambivalent in their relations with the United States, either because they disagree with specific aspects of U.S. policy (such as the Arab-Israeli conflict) or because they are constrained by anti-U.S. sentiment within their own populations.

Popular attitudes are even more complex and difficult to assess. The image of the United States as a "land of milk and honey" as well as a land of freedom and opportunity co-exists with another image of moral decadence and hostility to Islamic society in the minds of many residents of the Middle East. These conflicting images can lead to wide swings in popular attitudes toward the United States. The friendliness that many Americans encounter in casual contacts with ordinary citizens of Middle East countries can turn quickly to hostility and, on occasion, to violence when the United States adopts a policy seen by locals as inimical to Arab or Muslim interests.

This report will review the nature and evolution of attitudes toward the United States among Arabs and Muslims in the Middle East, discuss factors creating resentment toward the United States, and look briefly at the implications of various policies the United States might adopt to deal with these attitudes. Emphasis will be on attitudes in the Middle East, which remains the heartland of Arab and Muslim civilization. This area extends from Morocco in the west to Iran in the east, and comprises 18 Arabic-speaking countries (which are largely Muslim) and Iran (Muslim but not Arab). Israel, where the majority is neither Arab nor Muslim, is not covered, nor is Turkey, a Muslim country with a highly secular political system and a member of NATO. Also, this report does not deal primarily with several other Muslim countries located in southern or central Asia. Attitudes in these more distant Muslim countries, however, sometimes echo those encountered among Arabs and Muslims in the Middle East, albeit at a generally lower level of intensity.

EVOLUTION AND NATURE OF ATTITUDES

Historical Legacy

The United States fell heir to a complex relationship that developed between Islamic society and the west over a period of 14 centuries. Although the various Islamic empires that existed during that lengthy period were sometimes allied with one or more European states, Islamic-western relations tended to be a story of conflict: the early Arab conquests after the emergence of the Islamic religion; the European-led crusades from the 11th to 13th centuries; the expansion of the Ottoman Turkish empire into southeastern Europe in the 15th and 16th; and the establishment of colonial or quasi-colonial regimes over much of the Arab world by France, Britain, and to a lesser extent Italy in the 19th and early 20th. As Arab states acquired full independence following World War II, their citizens continued to harbor strong sensitivities over anything that suggested "western imperialism." Iran, occupied by Britain and the Soviet Union during World War II, retained similar sensitivities toward any form of interference from external powers.

The United States, a latecomer to the Middle East, enjoyed a more favorable image in the region than did its European counterparts in the 19th and early 20th centuries. With the brief exception of the Barbary wars, the United States was not involved in any regional conflict and had no discernable colonial ambitions in the region. U.S. visitors–mainly educators, travelers, and diplomatic envoys–were well received on the whole. A high point in regional perceptions of the United States may have been reached at the end of World War I, when inhabitants of the Middle East welcomed President Woodrow Wilson's call for self-determination and some of them saw in the United States a potential counterweight to the colonial ambitions of France and Britain.[1]

This period of minimal U.S. involvement in the Middle East came to an end after World War II, as the United States undertook expanded worldwide commitments and acquired three major interests in the Middle East region: maintaining access to the region's oil resources, blocking Soviet attempts to achieve hegemony in the Middle East, and safeguarding the security of the newly created state of Israel. Pursuit of these interests compelled the United States to

[1] In 1919, a congress of Syrian notables expressed the view that "the American Nation is farthest from any thought of colonization and has no political ambition in our country" and went on to state that it would request technical and economic assistance from the United States. Text is contained in J. C. Hurewitz, *Diplomacy in the Near and Middle East*, Volume II, Princeton, D. Van Nostrand Company, Inc., 1956, p. 63.

become an active player in Middle East affairs and adopt periodically conflicting policies that were sometimes resented in the region. In particular, the U.S. role in the creation of Israel in 1948 was decried among most Arabs and Muslims, who believed that a Palestinian state should have been set up in the disputed territory.

Moreover, in the decades that followed, U.S. policy collided with the two principal political movements in the region: secular pan-Arab nationalism, which was spread by the late Egyptian President Gamal Abdul Nasser, and Islamic fundamentalism, which began to replace secular nationalism in the 1970s.[2] Both movements to varying degrees developed anti-western and anti-Israeli underpinnings. A discussion of Islamic fundamentalist movements (sometimes referred to as Islamism, Islamic resurgence, or political Islam) is beyond the scope of this report; however, three points are worth noting. First, Islamic fundamentalism is not monolithic; it is espoused by a number of groups that vary in orientation and intensity. Second, the more militant fundamentalist groups with a penchant for violence have shown considerable drawing power among youth and lower middle classes. Third, the efforts of more extreme fundamentalists to undermine pro-U.S. regimes in the region, oppose Arab-Israeli peacemaking, and promote international terrorism have increasingly put Islamic fundamentalists at odds with the United States.[3]

Extent of Resentment

Attitudes toward the United States among Muslims and Arabs of the Middle East appear to be mixed. In the absence of reliable or consistent polling data, the extent and depth of opposition to the United States are hard to measure. Anecdotal evidence is varied and contradictory. One commentator, writing in the aftermath of the September 11 attacks, opined that "only a hard core of Muslim fanatics hates us enough to kill themselves and thousands of others ..."[4] Another commentator, while noting that the vast majority of Muslims and Arabs were shocked and horrified by the attacks, goes on to say that "a mood of resentment

---

[2] Non-Arab Iran had its own version of secular nationalism which was effectively stunted in 1953 when groups loyal to the late Shah led a counter-coup (with U.S. and British support) against the left-leaning Prime Minister Mohammed Mossadegh. Twenty-five years later Iran's leading Islamist, the late Ayatollah Rouhallah Khomeni, proved more successful in bringing about the overthrow of the Shah's pro-western regime.

[3] One commentator notes that "[s]ecularists, moderate Muslims, orthodox thinkers and extremists are proffering competing versions of Islam." Caryle Murphy, "A Hatred Rooted in Feelings," *The Washington Post*, September 16, 2001, p. B-1.

[4] Holger Jensen, "Here's Why They Hate Us," *The (Fairfax) Sunday Journal, October 28, 2001, p. A9.*

toward America" has become so commonplace in Middle East countries "that it was bound to breed hostility, and even hatred."[5] Contrasting viewpoints appear to exist side by side, and reflect long- standing ambivalence in regional attitudes toward the United States. Some individuals who express admiration for U.S. values such as freedom and opportunity often criticize aspects of American popular culture. Likewise, some who praise U.S. democracy may at the same time condemn U.S. policies on issues related to Israel and Iraq.

There are noteworthy differences between governmental attitudes and popular attitudes toward the United States, and some commentators believe that popular attitudes are winning out in their ability to influence regional policies. Most Middle East governments tend to see public opinion as a potential threat to the status quo. Friendly governments like those of Egypt, Jordan, and Saudi Arabia, are economically or strategically dependent on U.S. ties and will go to considerable lengths to support or acquiesce in U.S. policies even when they are domestically unpopular. Even less friendly governments, while using or instigating popular sentiment as a means of attacking specific U.S. policies, are uneasy over popular movements they see as threats to their regimes; Syria, for example, has long suppressed the fundamentalist Muslim Brotherhood. Both friendly and hostile governments, however, seem to feel increasingly constrained by popular attitudes. To an increasing extent, they are walking a fine line between attempting to control popular attitudes and seeking to coopt them.

Popular sentiment, on the other hand, operates under no such constraints. Often referred to as "the Arab street" (which loosely includes public opinion in non-Arab Iran as well), this popular sentiment has benefitted over the years from a steady expansion in the reach, availability, and sophistication of media outlets. In the late 1950s, the proliferation of transistor radios did much to spread the vision of Arab nationalism propagated by then Egyptian President Nasser. Twenty years later, cassette tapes enabled the late Ayatollah Rouhollah Khomeini to enlist supporters for his campaign to establish an Islamic republic in Iran. In recent years, the emergence of videotapes and satellite television has popularized Islamic fundamentalist views that in some cases have fueled outbreaks of terrorism. A political scientist in the Middle East observes that the Arab street is becoming increasingly Islamicized and adds: "The street counts."[6]

A key question which defies easy answers is the degree to which "the street" is hostile to the United States. The strongly Islamist orientation which seems to be a current feature of the street can easily be translated into anti-U.S. sentiment at

[5] Peter Ford, "Why do they hate us?", *The Christian Science Monitor*, September 27, 2001, p. 5.

[6] John Kifner, "The New Power of Arab Public Opinion," *New York Times*, November 11, 2001, Sec. 4, pp. 1,5.

the hands of skilled manipulators like Osama bin Laden. As explained below, U.S. policy has frequently been at variance with prevailing popular sentiment in the Middle East. A Saudi journalist, discussing the popular Qatar-based Al-Jazeera TV network, commented that "[t]hey know the taste of the Arab street, and the Arab street is anti-American."[7] Moreover, skepticism and a conspiratorial mentality among much of the population feed inflammatory theories that deepen popular distrust of the United States. For example, some Arab media have suggested that the September 11 attacks were carried out by the Bush Administration to solidify its hold on power.[8]

The street is not monolithic, however, and is probably not uniformly anti-American. Attitudes seem to vary according to the background and orientation of the individuals expressing them. There are indications that those who are most attracted to Islamic fundamentalism–for example, youth, poorer classes, some professionals and intellectuals–are more likely to view the United States in an unfavorable light. Conversely, ethnic and religious minorities such as the Kurds in Iraq and some Christians in Lebanon have long regarded western nations and particularly the United States as potential protectors against Arab or Muslim majorities. In Iran, in a curious reversal of popular sentiment, opinion leaders such as intellectuals and students are now reacting against the country's hard-line clerics, who remain among the most resolute opponents of the United States.[9] On balance, though, popular attitudes–at least among the most vocal groups–appear unfavorable toward the United States on a variety of issues.

LEADING ISSUES

The following discussion summarizes some of the leading issues that continue to stir resentment toward the United States among Arabs and Muslims in the Middle East. The list of issues is not exhaustive and the resentments that they arouse are not universally shared, but they are among the more commonly cited factors coloring regional attitudes toward the United States.

---

[7] Sharon Waxman, "Arab TV's Strong Signal," *The Washington Post*, December 4, 2001, p. C1.

[8] Warren Richey, "Muslim opinion sees a conspiracy," *The Christian Science Monitor*, November 6, 2001. The author quotes other conspiracy theories variously putting the blame for the September 11 events on Israeli intelligence, Japanese seeking to avenge Hiroshima and Nagasaki, McVeigh-type militia movements, or Chinese and Russians trying to block a U.S. missile shield.

[9] See, for example, Hugh Pope and Peter Waldman, "Iran's Islamic Leaders Face Sudden Unrest Since Terror Attacks," *The Wall Street Journal*, November 5, 2001, pp. A1,A10.

International and Economic Factors

As the lone remaining superpower, the United States has become a convenient target for complaint on a range of issues. Particularly in the Middle East, there is a sense that the United States can impose its will on international organizations and exercise military muscle in pursuing its objectives with little regard to the view of other countries. In summarizing Middle East attitudes, one observer writes that "[m]ost of the time, Washington does what it pleases in the region, paying little heed to criticism from Cairo or Riyadh or Amman. But then comes along an emergency, and suddenly the Americans expect Middle East governments to do our bidding."[10] Superpower envy on the part of Arabs and Muslims is not new; however, it has been heightened during the past decade by the absence of a second superpower which could act as a counterweight to unilateral action by the United States. At a more basic historical level, many Arabs and Muslims lament a world order in which there is no longer an overarching Muslim empire, which could balance other superpowers. They recall that such a Muslim empire had existed in one form or another from the early years of Islam until the collapse of the Ottoman Empire after World War I.[11]

From an economic standpoint, there is a sense of relative deprivation among large numbers of Arabs and Muslims in the Middle East. American affluence, widely seen by Middle East residents in western media broadcasts, is contrasted with privation in key segments of the Middle East population: Palestinian refugees, Yemeni villagers, urban underclasses in Egypt, and especially Iraqis struggling under a decade-old economic embargo. Even oil producing countries have seen some of their earlier prosperity erode as the oil market has become increasingly erratic; in Saudi Arabia, for example, per capita income has declined in real terms by as much as 50% since the early 1980s, with resulting cutbacks in social services.[12] Some in the region blame the United States for allegedly exerting pressure on oil producers to keep supplies plentiful and prices low.

---

[10] Steve Chapman, "Making friends and enemies in the Middle East," *Chicago Tribune*, September 20, 2001, p. 29.

[11] Fundamentalist zealots such as Osama bin Laden have exploited this resentment. In his taped message aired on October 7, 2001, bin Laden referred to humiliations visited upon the Muslim world "for more than 80 years." [Text in *The Washington Post*, October 2001, p. A12.] Historian Bernard Lewis believes this comment refers to the western role in overthrowing the Ottoman Empire, whose ruler carried the dual title of Sultan (temporal ruler) and Caliph (religious successor to the Prophet Muhammad).

[12] See Thomas Omestad, "The kingdom and the power," *U.S. News and World Report*, November 5, 2001, p. 34. According to DRI-WEFA, an econometric forecasting firm, per capita GDP declined in real terms from $12,681 in 1980 to $7,729 in 2000 (constant 1997 dollars). Some estimates show an even steeper decline.

Others question the seeming reluctance of U.S. business to invest in the Middle East.

These economic discontents may have been exacerbated by the phenomenon known as "globalization", defined by one source as "the integration of political, economic and cultural activities of geographically or nationally separated peoples."[13] One commentator observes that "[g]lobalization has caught it [the Middle East] at a bad demographic moment."[14] As the youthful population expands, growing numbers of young men compete for fewer opportunities in the traditional job market and often lack the skills to qualify for more technically sophisticated employment opportunities. The United States, seen as the vehicle of globalization, has become vulnerable to criticism from poorer classes and an increasingly alienated youth. In a public opinion poll of Palestinians conducted by Birzeit University (the leading university in the Israeli-occupied West Bank territory) in October 2001, 86.5% of respondents agreed with the statement that the United States is "[r]ich at the expense of poor nations."

Countervailing Considerations

The United States has shown restraint as a superpower, conducting military operations mainly to defend itself against terrorism (Operation Enduring Freedom in Afghanistan) defend vital economic interests (Operation Desert Storm against Iraq in 1991), or check widespread disorder and relieve famine (Operation Restore Hope in Somalia in 1993). In several cases it has deployed forces to protect Muslim communities, notably in Bosnia and Kosovo (as well as Afghanistan in the 1980s). During these military interventions, U.S. administrations have made a point of acting under U.N. Security Council resolutions. While seeking to replace avowedly hostile leaders like Saddam Hussein, the United States has not pursued a colonial vision or tried to establish long term military occupations in the Middle East.

Economic ills that affect much of the Middle East appear to result more from local policies than from the role of the United States. High birth rates, low productivity, unresponsive economic structures, and inadequate educational systems have retarded economic growth and kept countries in this region from becoming competitive in the international market. A financial expert on the

---

[13] For further definitions and discussion, see CRS Report RL30955, *The Issue of Globalization–An Overview*, May 3, 2001, by Gary J. Wells.

[14] Fareed Zakaria, "Why Do They Hate Us," *Newsweek*, October 15, 2001, p. 32.

Arabian Peninsula described the 1990s as a "lost decade" in the Middle East, noting that GDP growth had averaged about 1% throughout most of the region.[15]

In actuality, the United States has been a major benefactor of Arab and Muslim countries in the Middle East. Even if Israel is excluded, the United States has provided a disproportionate share of its foreign aid to Middle Eastern countries. In FY2001, the United States provided $2.396 billion in bilateral assistance to Arab and Muslim states in the Middle East, or 26% of total worldwide U.S. bilateral assistance ($9.199 billion). Since the inception of foreign assistance programs in 1946, the United States has provided $53.9 billion to Egypt, $5.1 billion to Jordan, and significant amounts to several other Middle East countries and groups in bilateral assistance. Some would argue, however, that at least a portion of this aid goes to strengthen existing regimes, which are not always popular (see below).

Unfavorable Images

For some years, there has been a widespread perception among Muslims in the Middle East that U.S. society is fundamentally alien, if not hostile, to Islamic beliefs and values. This perception is not confined to militant clerics; rather, it is shared by large numbers of people in the region. Critics tend to focus on problems in American society that often figure prominently in the media, such as the overuse of alcohol, drugs, and the breakdown of the traditional family. Many in the Middle East disapprove of American sexual mores, and American films and television shows are seen as promoting promiscuity. Western and particularly U.S. media are seen by some as a vehicle for corruption of Muslim society.

Arabs and other Muslims also complain that they are often unfairly portrayed in U.S. media. They cite caricatures appearing in American comic strips, cartoons, situation comedies, and movies as evidence of a built-in bias among Americans against their culture and beliefs. A scholar who researched Arab stereotypes in some detail stated that "the Arab remains a favorite whipping boy" and went on to list a number of contemporary TV programs which depicted Arabs in an unfavorable light.[16] In a similar vein, they object to the frequent use in the U.S. press of disparaging cliches and phrases, arguing for example that American

---

[15] Brad Bourland, Chief Economist, Saudi American Bank, speaking at a conference on Redefining U.S.-Arab Strategic Relations, held on September 9-10, 2001, under the sponsorship of the National Council on U.S.-Arab Relations in Washington, DC.

[16] Jack G. Shaheen, *The TV Arab*, Bowling Green, Ohio, Bowling Green State University Popular Press, 1984, pp. 122-123.

media too often link the word "terrorist" with "Arab," "Muslim," or "Palestinian." They maintain that U.S. media do not use such pre-judgmental phrases when dealing with terrorism perpetrated by groups outside the Muslim world. In the Birzeit poll, 88% of respondents believed that perceived American animosity toward Islam is a very important factor in shaping U.S.-Arab relations.

Countervailing Considerations

These criticisms, however widely felt, do not fully capture the ambivalence of Middle Eastern attitudes toward the United States. Many Arabs and Muslims in the Middle East, including those most critical of U.S. society and policy, are attracted to the democratic principles and economic opportunities that the United States has developed. Some find that the Sodom-Gomorrha label associated with the United States among many Middle Easterners does not generally apply. One commentator has noted that "America is easily the most religious of all the industrialized nations."[17] (Ironically, the less religious Europeans draw less criticism from the Muslim world.) For many years, long lines of visa applicants in front of U.S. embassies and consulates in Middle East countries have attested to the positive feelings that co-exist with negative impressions toward the United States.

A scientist from Yemen expressed some of this ambivalence about the United States in commenting that "[w]hen you go there, you really love the United States...You are treated like a human being, much better than in your own country. But when you go back home, you find the US applies justice and fairness to its own people, but not abroad."[18] In a similar vein, the Birzeit poll found that 66.5% of respondents believe the United States respects the human rights of its citizens and 52.6% believe it practices democracy within its borders; however, much lower percentages believe it promotes these values abroad (see below). An Egyptian actor, recounting a trip to the United States, said "I loved the American people." But he adds that "If you the Arab people to prove they love America, let America prove they love the Arab people."[19]

Observers have noted that some Middle Easterners secretly like the less conservative moral strictures they encounter in Euro-American societies and enjoy the very activities that many Muslim spokesmen decry. One commentator points out that Middle East residents themselves, not the United States, have

---

[17] Dan Morgan, "A Fervor Americans Can Recognize," *The Washington Post*, October 21, 2001, p. B1.

[18] Peter Ford, "Why do they hate us?," *The Christian Science Monitor*, September 27, 2001, p. 10.

[19] Sharon Waxman, "I Love You, Now Go Away," *The Washington Post*, December 17, 2001, pp. C1, C8.

created a demand for such cultural symbols of the United States as Coca-Cola, MTV, and blue jeans.[20]

Western Military Presence

The deployment of U.S. and other western military forces in the Middle East strikes a discordant note among many Arabs and other Muslims in the region. Since the U.S.-led coalition expelled Iraqi forces from Kuwait in 1991, the United States has maintained a force of approximately 25,000 military personnel in the Persian Gulf region, including approximately 5,000 in remote bases in Saudi Arabia. (The total figure has increased as the campaign against terrorism got under way in October 2001.) Many Arabs in the Middle East resent the presence of non-Muslim western forces, which evoke memories of European colonialism. In particular, the presence of western military forces on Saudi soil is seen by some as a desecration of the Islamic holy places of Mecca and Medina, which are located in Saudi Arabia. Significantly, the first grievance listed by Osama bin Laden in his *fetwa* (Muslim legal opinion) of February 1998 was the U.S. military presence in the Arabian Peninsula, and this complaint seems to have resonance in the region. Even some individuals and leaders who are less concerned with the U.S. military presence on religious grounds tend to suspect a long-term U.S. plan to maintain military bases in the Middle East.

The rulers of Saudi Arabia, torn between their need for western protection against renewed aggression by Iraq and their position as guardians of the Islamic holy sites, are sensitive to any discussion of their role in hosting U.S. military personnel. To a lesser extent, the same is true of the leaders of the smaller Gulf states who, like the Saudi leadership, are vulnerable to domestic and regional criticism from opponents of a U.S. military presence. (A partial exception is Kuwait, where memories of the seven-month Iraqi occupation and the U.S. role in terminating it are still fresh.) Consequently, Gulf leaders are reluctant to advertise any U.S. or other western use of bases on their territories, especially to launch allied strikes against targets in fellow Islamic states such as Iraq or more recently Afghanistan.[21]

---

[20] Michael Collins Dunn, "Trying to Get at the Whys," *The Estimate*, September 21, 2001, p. 2.

[21] A senior U.S. military official emphasized the importance of maintaining secrecy or "plausible deniability" when seeking to use facilities in Saudi Arabia. Vernon Loeb and Dana Priest, "Saudis Balk at U.S. Use of Key Facility," *The Washington Post*, September 22, 2001, pp. A1, A19.

Countervailing Considerations

The United States and its allies have made efforts to avoid offending Muslim sentiment or embarrassing friendly governments in the Middle East. President Bush and senior U.S. officials have repeatedly said the war against terrorism is not aimed at the Islamic religion. The U.S. military presence is generally unobtrusive. U.S. forces in Saudi Arabia, for example, are stationed at isolated locations at considerable distances from the Muslim holy sites of Mecca and Medina. All three U.S. administrations since the 1991 Gulf war have avoided detailed public discussion of U.S. troop locations, military deployments, or combat operations in an effort to avert criticism against Middle East countries hosting U.S. military contingents in the Persian Gulf region. Although many Arabs and Muslims opposed the U.S. campaign in Afghanistan, U.S. officials have stressed that most Afghans welcomed their liberation from the Taliban regime.

More broadly, the United States does not have a history of seeking a large-scale military presence in the Middle East. For many years, the United State maintained only an "over-the-horizon" presence consisting of a small naval force stationed in the Persian Gulf, despite the economic and strategic importance of that region. Even since the 1991 Gulf war, the United States has tried to minimize the need for stationing forces in the region through measures that do not require permanent deployment of troops. For example, the U.S. Armed Forces have prepositioned military equipment in several Gulf states for use in a contingency, engaged in combined military exercises, and carried out short term training missions. The United States has withdrawn from bases when requested to do so by a host government, as it did from Libya and Morocco in the 1970s. U.S. participation in regional peacekeeping operations, notably the Multinational Force and Observers established under the Egyptian-Israeli peace treaty of 1979, has elicited little or no opposition within the Middle East.

Containment Policy Toward Iraq

The U.S. role in implementing economic and military measures to contain Iraq has become increasingly unpopular in the Middle East. Regional reactions were mixed when Iraq invaded Kuwait in 1990, but Iraqi President Saddam Hussein's accompanying denunciation of oil rich regimes resonated among many ordinary citizens, especially in less affluent Middle East countries. Since the U.S.-led coalition expelled Iraqi forces from Kuwait in 1991, public opinion in the Middle East has increasingly blamed economic sanctions imposed by the U.N.

Security Council for the continuing hardships that the Iraqi people have suffered for the past ten years. The United States, widely seen as the principal force in maintaining sanctions, has drawn the lion's share of such criticism and is portrayed as insensitive to the plight of Iraqi citizens unable to obtain the basic necessities of life. As one commentator put it, "[w]hile many in the Arab world do not like Saddam Hussain, they believe that the United States has chosen a particularly inhuman method of fighting him–a method that is starving an entire nation."[22]

The U.S. and British role in the military aspects of containing Iraq is also a focus of criticism in the region. Since the early 1990s, both countries have conducted regular overflights of northern and southern Iraq to deter the regime from oppressing internal opposition groups or from threatening neighboring states. These overflights have resulted in frequent clashes as U.S. and British aircraft have responded to challenges from Iraqi air defense units, and Iraq asserts that allied strikes have inflicted significant collateral damage. On several occasions, most notably in December 1998 (Operation Desert Fox), the United States and Britain have conducted more extensive air strikes against major Iraqi installations. Even the leaders of friendly Arab states–Egypt, Saudi Arabia, and Jordan–have deplored the use of force against Iraq and the allied strikes have been decried in local media. On the "Arab street", reactions have been even more hostile. A popular conspiratorial theory holds that the United States–despite periodic military action against Iraq–actually wants to keep Saddam in power. According to this theory, "Saddam Hussein had been lured into Kuwait by an American green light–and then kept in power and let off the hook–so that Pax Americana would have the pretext for stationing its forces in the region."[23]

Of particular concern to many in the region is the possibility that the United States may expand the current campaign against Osama bin Laden and the Taliban to target Iraq or possibly other Muslim countries on the State Department's terrorism list (such as Iran, Syria, or Libya). At a meeting of the 56-member Organization of the Islamic Conference (OIC) on October 10, 2001, attendees refrained from criticizing the U.S. campaign against bin Laden/Taliban forces in Afghanistan but rejected the targeting of any other Arab or Muslim country. Key allies such as President Mubarak of Egypt and King Abdullah of Jordan have urged the United States not to take this step, which they think could cause a major backlash in their countries and elsewhere in the Middle East.

---

[22] Fareed Zakaria, "Why Do They Hate Us?," *Newsweek*, October 15, 2001, p. 36.

[23] Fouad Ajami, "The Sentry's Solitude," *Foreign Affairs*, November/December 2001, p. 11.

Countervailing Considerations

U.S. officials have consistently maintained that the economic ills that beset post-war Iraq are of Saddam's making. They point out that Saddam temporized for five years before grudgingly accepting a plan offered by the United Nations to purchase essential supplies for the Iraqi people with revenues from UN-supervised oil sales (the "oil-for-food" program). Since 1998, Iraq has been allowed to sell unlimited quantities of oil under this plan; however, a number of observers believe that Saddam's government has obstructed the intent of the plan by siphoning off up to $1.5 billion of these revenues per year to build palaces, reward key supporters of the regime, and finance military purchases.[24] Moreover the northeastern Kurdish region, which has enjoyed de facto independence from Iraq since 1991, is in much better economic shape than those parts of Iraq under Saddam's control, even through the Kurdish region is under the same sanctions regime. In the spring of 2001, the U.N. Security Council did not agree to a U.S.-sponsored plan to expedite humanitarian supplies to Iraq while interdicting goods with potential military uses. In November, however, the United States and Russia obtained Security Council agreement to raise this "smart sanctions" proposal again in 2002.

Regarding the military aspects of containment, U.S. administrations since 1991 have maintained that overflights to enforce no-fly zones over parts of Iraq are grounded in U.N. Security Council resolutions adopted after the 1991 Gulf war. (Not all U.N. members agree with this interpretation.) They discount the numbers of civilian casualties reported by Iraq and point out that in some cases Iraq has used civilians as human shields by emplacing air defense units near populated areas. More massive allied strikes were brought on by major Iraqi violations of cease-fire terms; in December 1998 (Operation Desert Fox), the four-day allied bombing campaign, took place after almost two years of mounting Iraqi interference with U.N. inspectors seeking to find and dismantle Iraqi programs for developing weapons of mass destruction.

U.S. officials believe it would be risky to terminate economic sanctions or military overflights in the absence of clear evidence that Iraq is prepared to honor its obligations to abandon weapons of mass destruction programs and refrain from oppressing internal groups, threatening neighbors, or supporting international terrorism. U.S. officials fear that Iraq may be exploiting the absence of any

---

[24] Colum Lynch, "US Agrees to Compromise on Trade Restrictions on Iraq," *The Washington Post*, November 28, 2001, p. A31; Carola Hoyos, "UN chief seeks to ease controls on Iraqi oil cash," *(London) Financial Times*, August 1, 2001, p. 7. Iraqi officials say the United States and Britain frequently place holds on contracts for essential civilian supplies ordered under the oil-for-food plan.

inspection regime since December 1998 to move forward with its weapons programs. An essential step in demonstrating good faith would be for Iraq to readmit U.N. weapons inspectors with full access to Iraqi installations in accordance with Security Council resolutions, as President Bush demanded during an interview on November 26, 2001.

U.S. Policy toward the Arab-Israeli Conflict

Perhaps the most frequently cited source of resentment against the United States among Arabs and Muslims is their conviction that U.S. policy regarding the Arab-Israeli conflict is biased toward Israel. Resentment is particularly strong among the Palestinian community: Palestinians in the West Bank and Gaza chafe under a 30-year-plus Israeli occupation; Palestinians in other countries feel that much of the world, including the United States, is indifferent to their plight. At present, two aspects of the long-festering Arab-Israeli problem are creating particular concerns in the Middle East. First, the collapse of U.S.-brokered Israeli-Palestinian negotiations in July 2000 led to an on-going Palestinian uprising (*intifada*), amid widespread Arab complaints that U.S. administrations have been unwilling to press Israel on key issues of Palestinian concern. Second, U.S.-sponsored talks between Israeli and Syrian representatives broke down during the same year, followed by continuing clashes in the Israeli-Lebanese-Syrian tri-border area.[25]

Feelings vary in intensity, but concern over this issue is not confined to the people directly involved, i.e., the Palestinians and Syrians. Palestinian efforts to achieve statehood, in particular, have long stirred emotions throughout the Middle East. According to a poll conducted in the summer of 2001 by a Middle East expert at the University of Maryland, nearly 60% of the people in four Arab countries–Saudi Arabia, Kuwait, the United Arab Emirates (UAE), and Lebanon–considered the Palestinian problem to be the single most important issue to them personally. An even higher percentage of Egyptians, 79%, gave the same answer.[26] This widespread preoccupation in the Middle East with the Palestinian issue often takes the form of animosity and violence against the United States,

[25] For further background on the Arab-Israeli conflict and recent efforts to resolve it, see CRS Issue Brief IB91137, *The Middle East Peace Talks*, by Carol Migdalovitz; CRS Issue Brief IB 92052, *Palestinians and Middle East Peace: Issues for the United States*, by Clyde Mark; and CRS Report RL31078, *The Shib'a Farms Dispute and Its Implications*, by Alfred B. Prados.

[26] The pollster, Professor Shibley Telhami, reviewed the results of his poll during his keynote speech at the Middle East Institute's 55th Annual Conference held in Washington, DC, ON October 19, 2001.

which is seen as Israel's principal supporter. The Birzeit poll indicated that 90% of Palestinians regard perceived U.S. bias toward Israel as a very important factor shaping U.S.-Arab relations. In addressing the many aspects of this conflict, Arab and Muslim interlocutors voice a series of long-standing complaints.

Perceived Leverage

Many Arabs and Muslims doubt that the United States is serious in pressing for a solution to the conflict. They believe that large-scale U.S. aid to Israel should have provided U.S. leaders with sufficient leverage to obtain concessions that would have led to an agreement on terms that Arab leaders could accept. Palestinians, in particular, believe the United States could influence Israel to relax onerous features of the occupation of the West Bank and Gaza and cease such activities as expansion of Jewish settlements in these territories.[27]

Consistency

Many Arabs and Muslims assert that the United States operates under a dual standard in which other countries are held to a stricter standard than Israel in meeting international obligations. They compare U.S. economic and military pressure on Iraq to honor the terms of U.N. resolutions with a seeming absence of pressure on Israel to comply with other U.N. resolutions or agreements that address occupation issues, the status of Jerusalem, and weapons of mass destruction. Similarly, they criticize U.S. silence regarding Israeli use of U.S.-supplied military equipment to strike populated areas in the West Bank, Gaza, and southern Lebanon.[28]

Terrorism Definition

Arabs and Muslims uniformly disagree with U.S. definitions of terrorism, which they believe unfairly target Palestinian and Lebanese groups seeking to end Israeli occupation of the West Bank and Gaza territories and (until May 2001) a

---

[27] Amr Moussa, Secretary General of the Arab League and former Egyptian Foreign Minister, enumerated some of the major Palestinian complaints: "As long as the Israeli government continues its policy of assassinations, building settlements, destroying homes and blockading towns, the violence will continue." Douglas Jehl, "Arabs Say It Was Israel That Set Off Cycle of Violence," *The New York Times*, December 4, 2001, p. A-8.

[28] On rare occasions, the United States has temporarily suspended military shipments to Israel over this issue. For further discussion, see CRS Report RL30982, *U.S. Defense Articles and Services Supplied to Foreign Recipients: Restrictions on Their Use*, May 30, 2001, by Richard F. Grimmett.

portion of southern Lebanon.[29] They maintain that the term "terrorism" should not be applied to "national resistance movements."

Countervailing Considerations

Since 1973, successive U.S. administrations have devoted intense efforts to the quest for a solution to the Arab-Israeli conflict. U.S. diplomacy played a major role in the conclusion of the Egyptian-Israeli peace treaty (1979), the Israeli-Jordanian peace treaty (1994), and a series of Israeli-Palestinian agreements that resulted in limited Palestinian self-rule over 70% of Gaza and approximately 40% of the West Bank in the 1990s. U.S. administrations have frequently pressed Israeli counterparts to take further steps in advancing the peace process. Many commentators believe Arabs in general and Palestinians in particular have missed numerous opportunities for a comprehensive peace settlement. In July 2000, after two weeks of U.S.-sponsored negotiations, Palestinian Chairman Yasir Arafat rejected a reported offer by then Israeli Prime Minister Ehud Barak to recognize a Palestinian state in over 90% of the West Bank and most of Gaza. Earlier that year, then Syrian President Hafiz al-Asad had rejected an Israeli offer to return virtually all of the Golan Heights territory, which Israeli had also occupied in the June 1967 Arab-Israeli war.

Both Arab leaders viewed Israel's proposals as insufficient. Asad insisted that Israeli withdrawal should be total (as it was with Egypt). Arafat argued that Barak had not offered contiguous territories to the Palestinians nor had he offered any Palestinian sovereignty in Jerusalem. In showing little flexibility, however, Arafat and Asad appear to have bypassed the most comprehensive offer any Israeli government is likely to make. Just before leaving office in February 2001, then Prime Minister Barak stressed that ideas raised during Israeli-Palestinian negotiations during the previous year were now null and void.[30]

Acts of terrorism perpetrated by extremists and the frequent failure of even mainstream Arabs and Muslims to condemn such acts have been an important factor in creating an unfavorable image of Arabs in general and Palestinians in particular. Among foreign terrorist groups designated by the Department of State under 1996 legislation, seven are Palestinian and four more represent other Arab groups (notably the Lebanese Shi'ite Muslim organization Hizballah). Of seven countries designated by the State Department as state sponsors of terrorism, five

---

[29] Lebanese argue that even the unilateral Israeli withdrawal from southern Lebanon in May 2000 was incomplete. For more information, see CRS Report RL31078, *The Shib'a Farms Dispute and Its Implications*, August 7, 2001, by Alfred B. Prados.

[30] "Barak, Powell discuss Palestinian issue, Russian technology transfer to Iran," *Voice of Israel*, Jerusalem, in English, 0500, February 25, 2001–BBC Monitoring.

are Arab or Muslim states in the Middle East. (Arabs and Muslims complain that the list is skewed to target Middle Eastern countries.)

More fundamentally, some experts on the region question the degree to which Arab-Muslim hostility toward the United States can be attributed to the Arab-Israeli conflict rather than to other grievances. Some of the most virulent outbursts of anti-American hostility, such as the seizure of the U.S. embassy by militant Iranian students in 1979 or the attacks on U.S. military facilities in Saudi Arabia in 1995 and 1996, have had little to do with U.S. support of Israel. Historian Bernard Lewis suggests that "resentment of Israel is the only grievance that can be freely and safely expressed in those Muslim countries where the media are either wholly owned or strictly overseen by the government. Indeed, Israel serves as a useful stand-in for complaints about the economic privation and political repression under which most Muslim people live, and as a way of deflecting the resulting anger."[31] To the extent that Middle East publics also blame the United States for these problems, Arab and Muslim hostility toward the United States might well continue, some argue, even if the Israeli-Palestinian problem were to be resolved.

U.S. Support for Unpopular Regimes

As noted earlier, attitudes toward the United States often differ on the governmental and popular levels. Ironically, long-standing U.S. support for various regimes in the Middle East in some cases has adversely affected the U.S. image among mainstream residents. Much of the "Arab street" is critical of U.S. support for governments that are perceived by some segments of the population as dictatorial, corrupt, narrowly based, or un-Islamic. These labels are variously applied to important U.S. allies including Egypt, Jordan, Morocco, Saudi Arabia, and Tunisia. Although these countries have opened their political systems to a degree, most of them face challenges from dissident elements often with an Islamic fundamentalist bent, and regularly use the coercive organs of the state to suppress dissent, even when it is non-violent. The United States draws blame from many in the region for its role in bolstering these regimes through political support, arms transfers, or financial aid.

Results of the Birzeit poll, which dealt with Palestinian public opinion, gave Arab regimes low marks, and these negative feelings are transferred by some to the United States. Only 18% thought Arab regimes practice democracy, 25%

---

[31] Bernard Lewis, "The Revolt of Islam," *The New Yorker*, November 19, 2001, p. 56.

thought they allow freedom of the press, and 27% thought they respect rights of citizens. Fifty-four percent of respondents described "perceived U.S. support of undemocratic regimes" as a very important factor in shaping U.S.-Arab relations. In a related criticism, only 22% and 17.8%, respectively, believe the United States promotes democracy and human rights around the world, although as mentioned above, respondents gave fairly high marks to U.S. performance at home. Dissatisfaction with U.S. ties to existing regimes, though hard to quantify, extends well beyond the Palestinian community. Dr. Lewis observes that Middle Easterners increasingly voice complaints not over U.S. ties to Israel "but something nearer home and more immediate–American complicity with corrupt tyrants who rule them."[32] There is some evidence that terrorist acts directed against U.S. targets are aimed primarily at Arab regimes that deal with the United States.[33]

Countervailing Considerations

Some commentators may overestimate the degree of popular anger at U.S. support of allied Middle Eastern regimes. Political systems in friendly Middle East countries, though not democratic by U.S. standards, are attuned in many respects to their societies. In Jordan, King Hussein and his successor King Abdullah have stayed in touch with their subjects through a network of personal and semi-official contacts.[34] In Saudi Arabia and other Gulf states, monarchs operate under a consultative or *shura* system which includes both advisory councils and mechanisms for rulers to hear the concerns of common citizens.[35] While critics have long questioned the legitimacy of Middle Eastern rulers, various factors have helped them retain a degree of popular acceptance: roots in a prestigious dynasty, as in Saudi Arabia, Jordan, and Morocco; developing

---

[32] Bernard Lewis, "The Revolt of Islam," *The New Yorker*, November 19, 2001, p. 56.

[33] After the bombing of a U.S. Air Force facility in the eastern Saudi town of Khobar in 1996, a young Saudi told a U.S. reporter that "I did not like it, but only for one reason: it hit only the Americans, when the target should have been the [Saudi] Government itself." Douglas Jehl, "Saudi's Heartland Is Seething With Rage at Rulers and U.S.," *The New York Times*, November 5, 1996, p. A1.

[34] Both kings have had a penchant for taking the peoples' pulse through incognito visits to government offices and other public facilities. Jeffrey Goldberg, "Learning How To Be King," *The New York Times Magazine*, February 6, 2000, pp. 43ff; King Hussein ibn Talal, *Uneasy Lies the Head*, London, xxx, p. x.

[35] As one commentator put it, "The Saudi royal family has long argued it has its own form of democracy in the tradition of the *majlis*, or "sitting," when subjects are allowed into palace reception halls to press petitions on princes–and often the king himself." Nora Boustany, "Saudis' New Consulting Council Speaks to King in Muted Tones," *The Washington Post*, August 19, 1994, p. A30.

constitutional procedures (Jordan, Egypt, Morocco, Kuwait); and innovative political reforms (Bahrain, Qatar, Oman).

Most friendly Middle East governments have weathered numerous political crises and do not appear on the verge of collapse. Rather, they have provided a degree of stability which has furthered U.S. strategic, political, and economic objectives in the region. Moreover, they have acted as counterweights to radical regimes in the Middle East and in some cases as intermediaries between the United States and such regimes, notably Syria. U.S. economic, military, or political support for these friendly states demonstrates to less friendly leaders that alignment with the United States carries practical advantages. The dramatic reorientation of Egyptian policy under the late President Anwar Sadat in the 1970s remains a powerful example of the attraction of a good bilateral relationship with the United States.

IMPLICATIONS

Issues that affect Arab and Muslim attitudes toward the United States are long-standing features of U.S. relations with the Middle East. It is unlikely that resolution of any one of these issues by itself would usher in a new era of U.S.-Muslim amity or avert possible attacks on the United States or its interests. Various remedies have been suggested to deal with problems in U.S.-Middle Eastern relationships, but such suggestions are not panaceas. One commentator, discussing some of the causes of U.S.-Middle Eastern friction and the September 11 terrorist attacks, observes that "[n]one of this [discussion] is to give into to the simplistic response some have made: that if the US changed this or that policy, this would not have happened."[36] It may be possible, however, to mitigate hostility among many inhabitants of the Middle East through a careful review of the most common irritants in U.S. relations with the countries and people of this region.

Listed below are several illustrative steps that U.S. policy-makers could consider in dealing with issues enumerated above, together with a brief discussion. These steps are not mutually exclusive and in some cases could be pursued in combination. Implicit in each step is the option to reverse course if rapidly changing developments in the Middle East scene should so dictate.

---

[36] Michael Collins Dunn, "Trying to Get at the Whys," *The Estimate*, September 21, 2001, p. 2.

- Continue attempts to bridge economic inequities through aid and trade programs.

Current threats to worldwide U.S. interests and the need for stable friendly regimes to cooperate with U.S. efforts in the Middle East may argue for some incremental increases in aid to countries like Egypt, Jordan, and other less affluent regional states. (At present, economic aid to Egypt is being reduced to half its 1998 level under a phased ten-year program.) Such increases might enhance internal stability by providing short term help to these governments in dealing with hardships brought on by austerity measures needed to reform their economies. However, according to a counter-argument, bilateral government-to-government aid is sometimes subject to waste or abuse and runs the risk of further alienating elements of the "Arab street" that view their governments unfavorably. An alternative approach might be trade enhancements, such as conclusion of a free trade agreement with Egypt and support for Saudi Arabia's candidacy for membership in the World Trade Organization. Another approach might be encouragement of increased humanitarian support from the U.S. private sector. Another alternative might be to make economic aid conditional on steps by recipient regimes to encourage greater transparency and rectitude in government.

- Try to counter unfavorable images.

U.S. public diplomacy programs could be expanded in an effort to help counter perceptions of the United States as a center of vice and anti-Islamic sentiment and to explain U.S. objectives in fighting terrorism and seeking peace in the Middle East. A commentator has noted that "the administration has struggled with finding Arab and non-Arab Islamic allies to speak to the region on America's behalf."[37] Fledgling efforts by the administration like the appearance of an Arabic-speaking former U.S. ambassador on the popular Arabic TV channel *al-Jazeera* may represent a new and fruitful approach in reaching a wider audience in the Middle East. Some observers, however, question the efficacy of satellite television in attracting Middle East viewers and suggest concentrating more on broadcast TV and several newspapers with wide circulation.[38] Other potentially fruitful approaches might be to expand State Department speakers' programs and people-to-people exchanges. A long-term effort to expand U.S. informational

---

[37] Michael R. Gordon, "U.S. Tries To Rally Public Support Overseas," *The New York Times*, November 6, 2001, p. A1.

[38] One notes that only 10% of Arabs have satellite dishes. Mamoun Fandy, "To Reach Arabs, Try Changing the Channel," *The Washington Post*, December 2, 2001, p. B2.

programs in the Middle East is likely to proceed gradually since there are many obstacles, including a limited pool of linguists, competing demands for resources, and ingrained skepticism toward the United States, among much of the target audience.

- Seek wider backing for U.S. policies toward Iraq.

The ten-year-old embargo against Iraq has become increasingly unpopular in the Middle East as sympathy for the plight of the Iraqi people has grown throughout the region. A renewed U.S. effort to replace current trade restrictions with a regime of "smart sanctions" that would broaden the range of products available to the Iraqi people could ease a serious irritant in U.S. relations with Middle East states, particularly Jordan, whose economy is linked in many ways to that of Iraq. Russia, the principal obstacle to a previous U.S. effort to modify sanctions, appears to have dropped its objections.[39] Sanctions revision, however, would not be a viable option if Iraq were linked to the September 11 attacks or to the subsequent cases of anthrax. Also, Iraq's continued challenges to U.S. and British enforcement of no-fly zones is likely to ensure continued allied retaliatory strikes, which are not popular in the Middle East.

- Consider a new framework for Arab-Israeli peace negotiations.

Former mechanisms for Arab-Israeli negotiations set up during the George H. W. Bush and Clinton Administrations largely evaporated as talks foundered and violence increased in 2000. Further progress in the current campaign against terrorism might offer a fresh opportunity to reinvigorate negotiations, as former President Bush did in the aftermath of the 1991 Gulf war. Many regard the Arab-Israeli conflict as a leading source of discontent and potential unrest among citizens of several Middle East countries; they argue that an increased U.S. effort to resolve this conflict could decrease internal threats to Arab regimes and make them more willing to cooperate with other U.S. regional endeavors. Others are more skeptical, pointing out that popular opposition to the United States results not only from local perceptions of U.S. bias toward Israel but from other factors described above. They also point out that the parties failed to reach agreement on key issues despite a major expenditure of time and energy by both previous

[39] On November 29, 2001, Russia voted for U.N. Security Council Resolution 1382, which provides for the implementation in May 2002 of a "Goods Review List" that will facilitate most shipments to Iraq while blocking military or dual use items.

administrations. They doubt that the United States should devote extensive resources to another peacemaking endeavor until there is a reasonable assurance of success.

- Encourage more open political systems within the Middle East.

A weak link in U.S. efforts to establish a more stable and productive relationship with Arab and Muslim countries in the Middle East is the gap between the "Arab street" and the governing regimes, which are often regarded as being out of touch with popular sentiment. Over the past few years, a younger generation of rulers have made limited attempts to open their political systems to wider participation. Several traditional monarchies in the smaller Gulf states, for example, are moving toward elected parliaments. The United States might find it beneficial to encourage these trends in friendly Middle East countries. U.S. officials could point out that by tolerating dissent and creating more democratic institutions with greater accountability, these governments could provide a safety valve that might lessen challenges from opposition groups. This would have to be done with care, however, to avoid the appearance of U.S. interference in the political life of regimes already vulnerable to criticism by opponents of their U.S. ties. More fundamentally, U.S. policy makers may find it prudent to weigh the benefits of encouraging a more open political system against the risks of a takeover by political groups that oppose U.S. objectives in the Middle East.[40]

Resentment toward the United States within the Middle East may be part of the landscape for some time to come. It will probably continue to ebb and flow as it has done in the past, and the more dramatic manifestations of this hostility are likely to be the exception rather than the rule. Current issues, including the ones examined in this report, may metamorphose or be replaced by others over time. Even if these issues do not lend themselves to ready solution, an understanding of them can help signal the likelihood of potential threats to the United States or its interests. Moreover, U.S. cooperation with selected countries of the Middle East is of long standing, and it is likely that a fund of good will toward the United States

[40] A U.S. scholar and former diplomat opines that "[m]ore Islamists, imbued with a congenital hatred for Israel...would doubtless be elected" if unfettered elections were held in Jordan. Hermann Frederick Eilts, "Islamic Fundamentalism: A Quest for a New Order," *Mediterranean Quarterly*, Fall 1990, p. 36.

still exists within various Arab and Muslim circles in the Middle East. Historical cooperation and residual good will may provide a basis for more positive relationships in the years ahead.

INDEX

Y